BRICK BY BRICK

DINOSAURS

WARREN ELSMORE

BRICK BY BRICK
DINOSAURS

WARREN ELSMORE

RP|KIDS
PHILADELPHIA

Running Press Kids
Hachette Book Group
1290 Avenue of the Americas, New York, NY 10104
www.runningpress.com/rpkids
@RP_Kids

Printed in China

Originally published in 2017 by Weldon Owen, an imprint of Kings Road Publishing in the U.K.
First U.S. Edition: May 2018

Published by Running Press Kids, an imprint of Perseus Books, LLC, a subsidiary of Hachette Book Group, Inc.

The Hachette Speakers Bureau provides a wide range of authors for speaking events. To find out more, go to www.hachettespeakersbureau.com or call (866) 376-6591.

The publisher is not responsible for websites (or their content) that are not owned by the publisher.

LEGO, the LEGO logo, the Brick and Knob configurations, and the Mini-figure are trademarks of the LEGO group, which does not sponsor, authorize, or endorse this book.

Print book cover and interior design by Gareth Butterworth and Emma Vince
Edited by Fay Evans, Hazel Erikkson, and Claudia Martin

Library of Congress Control Number: 2017952997

ISBNs: 978-0-7624-9147-6 (flexi-bind), 978-0-7624-9146-9 (ebook), 978-0-7624-9237-4 (ebook), 978-0-7624-9236-7 (ebook)

WKT

10 9 8 7 6 5 4 3 2 1

CONTENTS

INTRODUCTION

WELCOME TO *BRICK BY BRICK: DINOSAURS!*

Dinosaur *loosely translates as "terrible lizard" in ancient Greek.*

Everyone knows that dinosaurs were some of the largest animals to ever walk the Earth. But did you know that some were just the size of a modern-day chicken? Or that some dinosaurs never really left us and still roam the Earth today? With such variety, where do we even start when writing a book on LEGO® dinosaurs?

When I started to think about this book, a few things became very obvious. First, dinosaurs aren't an easy thing to build in LEGO® bricks. They have curved, organic shapes that bring some new challenges.

Second, they need to be very well balanced. Without muscles and tendons to support them, our LEGO® dinosaurs might need some help standing up! Finally, we realized that we'd need some real expert help. How did dinosaurs grow? What sizes, shapes, and colors were they? How did they move? Which LEGO® pieces would be best to re-create the body parts of animals that died millions of years ago?

The answer was to put together a really great team to help bring dinosaurs to life in bricks. Working with a real paleontologist (an expert in dinosaurs) and some fantastic LEGO®

Though we've included a couple of full builds of skeletons in our book, it's incredibly rare to find a complete dinosaur skeleton. One of the most complete skeleton fossils ever found is a T.rex—it is 90 percent complete, and named Sue after the paleontologist who found it.

builders, we first picked our favorite dinosaurs to build. There were some obvious choices, of course. The Triceratops and Brontosaurus jumped out straight way—but how would we build the armored plates of a Stegosaurus?

With our dinos selected, it was time to work out how they might look in LEGO® bricks. With many of them being hugely different in scale, we decided we'd make each model look as good as we could –even if that does mean that some of them are a bit larger than the others! For instance, the Brachiosaurus model has turned out to be smaller than the Archaeopteryx, as it has a less complicated shape.

Once we knew which dinosaurs to build and were able to construct them in whatever size worked best, it was time to put the bricks together. In this book are instructions to build seventeen dinosaurs and other prehistoric creatures at home. We've tried to use mainly bricks you might

already have, but a word of warning: dinosaurs were BIG, so some of these instructions are among the most complicated I've ever written. Don't worry if you don't have exactly the right bricks to build all these dinosaurs as there are lots to choose from.

I do hope this book gives you the inspiration to have a go at building some dinosaurs of your own at home. One thing I learned from writing *Brick by Brick: Dinosaurs* is that a lot of facts about dinosaurs are simply still unknown. A lot of guesswork is involved! So whether you build a dinosaur that's as accurate as possible or one that's simply from your imagination, you can be sure of one thing: whatever you can imagine might have been real!

BRICK BASICS

The basic building elements are the brick and the plate (shown right) that come in many sizes, but some of the most useful LEGO® pieces for building the dinosaurs in this book are hinges. Hinges come in many sizes and shapes (see below). Keep lots of these handy!

Brick, 2 x 2

Plate

Technic
Axle Towball

Plate, Modified 1 x 2
with Towball and Small
Towball Socket on Ends

Plate, Modified 1 x 2
with Small Towball
Socket on Side

Plate, Modified 1 x 2
with Towball on Side

Plate, Modified 1 x 2
with Small Towball
Socket on End

Plate

Brick, Modified 2 x 2
with Ball Receptacle
Wide and Axle Hole

Brick, Modified 2 x 2
with Ball and Axle Hole
with 6 Holes in Ball

Plate, Modified 1 x 2
with Clip Horizontal
on End

Plate, Modified 1 x 2
with Handle on End—
Closed Ends

Plate, Modified 1 x 2
with Clips Horizontal
(Thick Open O Clips)

Plate, Modified 1 x 1
with Clip Horizontal
(Thick Open O Clip)

Plate, Modified 1 x 2
with Handle on Side—
Free Ends

Plate, Modified 1 x 1
with Clip Vertical—Type
4 (Thick Open O Clip)

Plate, Modified 1 x 2
with Angled Handles
on Side

Plate, Modified 1 x 2
with Clip on Top

The first dinosaur to be described as such was a Megalosaurus found in 1824.

builders, we first picked our favorite dinosaurs to build. There were some obvious choices, of course. The Triceratops and Brontosaurus jumped out straight way—but how would we build the armored plates of a Stegosaurus?

With our dinos selected, it was time to work out how they might look in LEGO® bricks. With many of them being hugely different in scale, we decided we'd make each model look as good as we could—even if that does mean that some of them are a bit larger than the others! For instance, the Brachiosaurus model has turned out to be smaller than the Archaeopteryx, as it has a less complicated shape.

Once we knew which dinosaurs to build and were able to construct them in whatever size worked best, it was time to put the bricks together. In this book are instructions to build seventeen dinosaurs and other prehistoric creatures at home. We've tried to use mainly bricks you might

already have, but a word of warning: dinosaurs were BIG, so some of these instructions are among the most complicated I've ever written. Don't worry if you don't have exactly the right bricks to build all these dinosaurs as there are lots to choose from.

I do hope this book gives you the inspiration to have a go at building some dinosaurs of your own at home. One thing I learned from writing *Brick by Brick: Dinosaurs* is that a lot of facts about dinosaurs are simply still unknown. A lot of guesswork is involved! So whether you build a dinosaur that's as accurate as possible or one that's simply from your imagination, you can be sure of one thing: whatever you can imagine might have been real!

BRICK BASICS

The basic building elements are the brick and the plate (shown right) that come in many sizes, but some of the most useful LEGO® pieces for building the dinosaurs in this book are hinges. Hinges come in many sizes and shapes (see below). Keep lots of these handy!

Brick, 2 x 2

Plate, 2 x 2

Technic, Axle Towball

Plate, Modified 1 x 2 with Towball and Small Towball Socket on Ends

Plate, Modified 1 x 2 with Small Towball Socket on Side

Plate, Modified 1 x 2 with Towball on Side

Plate, Modified 1 x 2 with Small Towball Socket on End

Plate, Modified 2 x 2 with Towball

Brick, Modified 2 x 2 with Ball Receptacle Wide and Axle Hole

Brick, Modified 2 x 2 with Ball and Axle Hole with 6 Holes in Ball

Plate, Modified 1 x 2 with Clip Horizontal on End

Plate, Modified 1 x 2 with Handle on End— Closed Ends

Plate, Modified 1 x 2 with Clips Horizontal (Thick Open U Clips)

Plate, Modified 1 x 2 with Handle on Side— Closed Ends

Plate, Modified 1 x 1 with Clip Horizontal (Thick Open O Clip)

Plate, Modified 1 x 2 with Handle on Side— Free Ends

Plate, Modified 1 x 1 with Clip Vertical—Type 4 (Thick Open O Clip)

Plate, Modified 1 x 2 with Angled Handles on Side

Plate, Modified 1 x 2 with Clip on Top

Plate, Modified 2 x 2 with Bar Frame Octagonal

WHERE TO FIND YOUR BRICKS

Most of us have some LEGO® bricks tucked away somewhere, whether in the attic or under the spare bed, and they're a great place to start to build some of the models in this book or your own prehistoric beasts! If you don't have any LEGO® around though (or the right piece!) then don't worry—it is possible to buy just the bricks you might need.

The first place to check is your local toy shop, and there are certain sets to look out for that will help you boost your LEGO® collection. The "LEGO® Classic" kits are full of useful bricks as well as a wonderful selection of basic bricks and plates too. These are great to build almost anything.

If you need specific LEGO® pieces, it's best to turn to the Internet. The LEGO website has a broad section called "Pick a Brick" at http://shop.lego.com/en-US/Pick-a-Brick. Here you can choose which bricks you want by color or type and order individual bricks. LEGO® doesn't list every single brick, but most of the bricks that we've used are listed here.

If you need a brick that LEGO® doesn't list on their website, perhaps an older or more rare brick, then it's best to turn to some of the other available websites that sell LEGO® bricks. The oldest of these with the largest selection is www.bricklink.com, though there are also newer sites available, like www.brickowl.com. These websites are somewhat like "eBay for LEGO®"! Individual sellers from around the world list the bricks they have for sale and you can select which ones to buy. Just be careful—it's addictive!

HOW TO USE THIS BOOK

The "Pieces Required" lists have every type of brick (and how many) that you will need for each build.

Each of the projects is broken down into numbered steps, with the pieces you need for each step shown in colored boxes.

When the step is more complicated, it has been broken down into a sub-step. This is where you will need to create a sub-build (or multiple sub-builds) to add onto what you have built so far. For example, you may have built the body of a dinosaur and a sub-step will detail how to create a leg, which then needs to be attached. In this example, an icon will let you know when you need to make more than one leg.

TECHNIQUES

If you want to build some of these dinosaurs at home, then there are some essential bricks and important techniques that you should know. It's not impossible to build your own dinosaurs without them, but they will really help!

Corresponding ball-and-socket and clip-and-bar joint pieces.

HINGES

As dinosaurs have movable limbs (like most living creatures), the key bricks to use for these builds are ones that let us re-create the animals' joints. There are two types of joint in particular:

The first joint that we've re-created is a ball-and-socket joint, just like the ones in your own hips or shoulders. Thankfully, LEGO® has quite a selection of ball-and-socket joints that we can use. Many of these pieces were introduced with the "Mixels" line of LEGO® sets, but some have been around for a very long time. There are two sizes of ball-and-socket joint, and for all but the very largest dinosaurs, the smaller joints, work just fine, which is handy because these are the easier parts to find!

The second joint we use still provides movement but also helps to make connections between body parts much stronger. This is the hinge joint—like the ones in your knees. While LEGO® does make specific hinge pieces, in most of our models we've used "clips" and "bars" to make hinge joints. These parts have the advantage of being available in a wide range of sizes and colors, so we don't need to worry about how to fit them into a model!

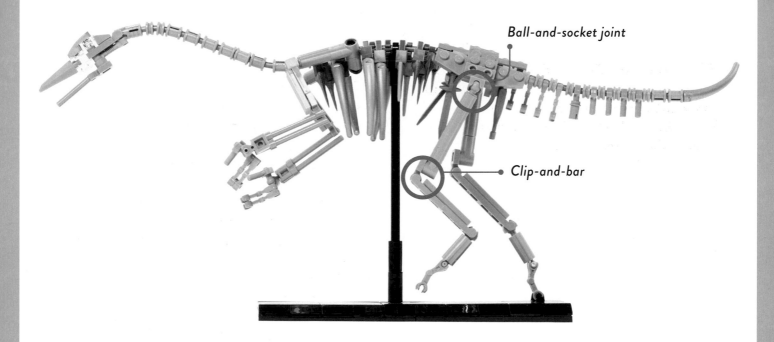

Ball-and-socket joint

Clip-and-bar

You might notice that many of the dinosaurs in this book include bricks that are built not only upward, but also sideways, and even backward. Like all animals, dinosaurs aren't square, so when it comes to building them in LEGO®, we needed to work out how to re-create their curves and muscles. The answer to this was to build with a technique known as SNOT! Not by putting bricks together with some sticky substance, but by building with Studs Not On Top. This is a technique that LEGO® fans have been using for a long time, and you have probably already used it without even noticing. Have you ever put headlights onto a car facing forward? Well, that's SNOT-work right there!

In our dinosaurs, we've built the sides of the dinos facing outward as this lets us use many of the curved bricks that LEGO® produces. Rather than being restricted to curves going just up and down, placing these bricks sideways lets us curve left and right. This is really important when using some colors of slopes, as the matching "inverted" part might not exist. By turning the bricks upside down, we can solve that problem without needing to add in strange colors. (Of course, dinosaur colors aren't actually known, so you can use whichever colors you like!)

PROJECTS

AGE OF THE DINOSAURS

Dinosaurs first walked the Earth around 230 million years ago. For many millions of years, they were the largest and most widespread land animals. Then, around 66 million years ago, most dinosaurs died out.

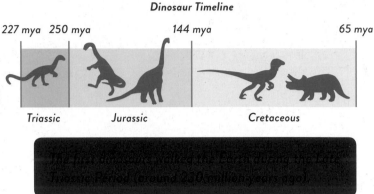

Dinosaur Timeline

227 mya   250 mya   144 mya   65 mya

Triassic   Jurassic   Cretaceous

The first dinosaurs walked the Earth during the Late Triassic Period (around 230 million years ago).

DINOSAURS EMERGE

The Earth is 4.5 billion years old, but for perhaps the first billion years, there was no life on our planet at all. The early Earth was baking hot and cloaked with poisonous gases. When the planet had cooled, the first life appeared in the oceans. These were simple organisms smaller than the head of a pin—in fact, they were microscopic! Over millions of years, water-living animals grew more complex and developed many different forms. Around 360 million years ago, the first amphibians

crawled onto land. They were the first four-legged vertebrates (animals with backbones). Amphibians live both in water and on land. Today's amphibians include frogs and newts.

After another 60 million years, the earliest reptiles evolved from amphibians. Reptiles were the first vertebrates to live their entire lives on land. Like today's reptiles, early reptiles laid hard-shelled eggs on land, had lungs to breathe air, and leathery skins. During the period that scientists call the Triassic Period, a special group of reptiles evolved: the dinosaurs. The dinosaurs (meaning "terrible lizards" in ancient Greek) walked in a new and very efficient way: with their legs held straight underneath their bodies. Other early reptiles, and reptiles such as

Trilobites roamed the oceans for more than 250 million years, with the first specimens believed to have appeared 500 million years ago. They eventually disappeared during another mass extinction event.

lizards today, walked with their legs sprawled out to the sides, which allows them to move much slower. Although other reptiles were usually little creatures, some dinosaurs evolved to be more than 100 feet (30 m).

MYSTERIOUS EXTINCTION

During the Jurassic and Cretaceous Periods, which followed the Triassic, dinosaurs flourished, evolving many different body forms, sizes, diets, and behaviors. All other land animals were small, usually much smaller than a modern cat, and lived in limited habitats. At least 1,000 different species of dinosaurs could be found across the entire globe. Then, around 66 million years ago, there was a catastrophe, marking the end of what is known as the Cretaceous Period.

Many scientists think that a massive asteroid struck the Earth, throwing up a cloud of dust that blocked out sunlight for many years. Evidence for this is a 112-mile (180-km)-wide crater structure in the rocks beneath the Gulf of Mexico, Central America. Without sunlight, many plants died, followed by lots of plant-eaters and the meat-eaters that preyed on them. Around three-quarters of all species became extinct. All the dinosaurs died, apart from the group of feathered dinosaurs that had evolved wings and taken to the skies—the birds. Modern birds are descendants of dinosaurs.

PREHISTORIC PROFILES

Hundreds of millions of years before the dinosaurs walked the Earth, many creatures lived during a time called the Carboniferous Period. At this time, the low-lying regions of the Earth were covered in humid swamps and rain forests that became a home to amphibians, reptiles, and large insects. Larger reptiles evolved as the Earth got hotter and dryer and eventually became the first dinosaurs.

Though people have been finding fossils and fossilized dinosaur bones for hundreds of years, the first named dinosaur was specified in 1824. It was the Megalosaurus, which means, "great lizard." More than 700 dinosaur species have been discovered and named since then, and paleontologists believe there are many more still to be found.

Some dinosaurs were bigger than buses, and others were as small as chickens, but dinosaurs of all sizes had a lot of things in common. They all walked with their legs directly under their bodies, and they were the only reptiles ever to do this. They laid eggs, and while most had scaly skin, many also had feather-like coverings.

MEGANEURA

Related to present-day dragonflies, the Meganeura lived during the Carboniferous Period, about 80 million years before the first dinosaurs emerged. It is thought that these insects were able to grow so large because the atmosphere at the time contained a lot more oxygen than our current atmosphere. Its name is pronounced meg-an-eoo-rah.

NAME: MEGANEURA

LIVED: NORTH AMERICA, FRANCE, GREAT BRITAIN

DIET: CARNIVORE

WINGSPAN: 25 IN (65 CM)

TRILOBITE

Trilobites were arthropods, which are animals without backbones that instead have an external skeleton and a segmented body. Modern arthropods include insects, spiders, and crustaceans, such as crabs. Trilobites evolved around 520 million years ago and flourished in the seas until 250 million years ago. Many trilobite fossils have been found. Trilobites ranged in size from 0.12 in (3 mm) to 12 in (30 cm). Trilobite is pronounced try-loh-bite.

NAME: TRILOBITE

LIVED: WORLDWIDE

DIET: VARIED, DEPENDING ON SPECIES

LENGTH: BETWEEN 0.12 IN (3 MM) AND 12 IN (30 CM)

WEIGHT: POSSIBLY UP TO 10 LB (4.53 KG)

PARASAUROLOPHUS

This duckbill dinosaur, a member of the Hadrosauridae family, lived in the late Cretaceous Period. It was found in warm, swampy regions of North America. Parasaurolophus had a hollow head crest and a duck-like mouth with hundreds of plant-grinding teeth. It grew up to 36 feet (11 m) long. Its name is pronounced par-a-sore-oh-loaf-us.

NAME: PARASAUROLOPHUS

LIVED: NORTH AMERICA

DIET: HERBIVORE

LENGTH: 36 FT (11 M)

WEIGHT: 7,700 LB (3,500 KG)

CORYTHOSAURUS

This ornithischian dinosaur was a member of the Hadrosauridae family, also known as duckbills. They were named for their flattened duck-like mouths. Corythosaurus lived in the late Cretaceous Period, around 75 million years ago, in North America. It grew to 33 feet (10 m) long. Its name is pronounced koh-ree-thoh-saw-rus.

NAME: CORYTHOSAURUS

LIVED: NORTH AMERICA

DIET: HERBIVORE

LENGTH: 33 FT (10 M)

WEIGHT: 9,920 LB (4,500 KG)

TRICERATOPS

Triceratops was a late Cretaceous Period dinosaur, living about 70 to 66 million years ago in North America. It was a member of the ornithischian group and the plant-eating Ceratopsidae family, known for their beaks, plant-grinding teeth toward the back of the jaw, horns, and neck frills. Triceratops grew up to 30 feet (9 m) long. Its name is pronounced try-ser-ah-tops.

NAME: TRICERATOPS

LIVED: NORTH AMERICA

DIET: HERBIVORE

LENGTH: 30 FT (9 M)

WEIGHT: 12,125 LB (5,500 KG)

ALETOPELTA

Living in Late Cretaceous North America, Aletopelta was an ornithischian dinosaur. It was part of the Ankylosauridae family of plant-eaters with broad bodies covered with bony plates, leaf-shaped teeth, short snouts, and tail clubs. It grew to be 20 feet (6 m) long and 16 feet (5 m) wide. Its name is pronounced al-ee-toh-pel-tuh.

NAME: ALETOPELTA

LIVED: NORTH AMERICA

DIET: HERBIVORE

LENGTH: 20 FT (6 M)

WEIGHT: 12,125 LB (5,500 KG)

STEGOSAURUS

Stegosaurus lived in the Late Jurassic Period, in western North America and Portugal. It was an ornithischian dinosaur and a member of the Stegosauridae family, which were four-legged plant-eaters with bony plates along their backs. Stegosaurus grew up to 30 feet (9 m) long. Its name is pronounced steg-oh-saw-rus.

NAME: STEGOSAURUS

LIVED: NORTH AMERICA

DIET: HERBIVORE

LENGTH: 30 FT (9 M)

WEIGHT: 6,800 LB (3,100 KG)

SPINOSAURUS

Spinosaurus (meaning "spine lizard" in ancient Greek) was a theropod dinosaur, part of the saurischian group. It was in the Spinosauridae family, which was made up of large predators with long crocodile-like skulls and cone-shaped teeth. Spinosaurus lived in the Cretaceous Period, from around 112 to 97 million years ago. Its name is pronounced spine-oh-saw-rus.

NAME: SPINOSAURUS

LIVED: NORTH AFRICA

DIET: CARNIVORE

LENGTH: 59 FT (18 M)

WEIGHT: 8,800 LB (4,000 KG)

BRACHIOSAURUS

Brachiosaurus was a sauropod dinosaur in the saurischian group. It was in the Brachiosauridae family of plant-eaters with gigantic bodies and long necks. Unlike other sauropods of the Jurassic Period, the brachiosaurus (from the ancient Greek for "arm lizards") had longer front legs than back legs and a shorter tail. Brachiosaurus lived in both North America and Africa. Its name is pronounced brak-ee-oh-saw-rus.

NAME: BRACHIOSAURUS

LIVED: NORTH AMERICA

DIET: HERBIVORE

LENGTH: 85 FT (26 M)

WEIGHT: 123,500 LB (56,000 KG)

DIPLODOCUS

Diplodocus lived in North America in the Late Jurassic Period, around 154 to 152 million years ago. It was a plant-eating sauropod in the Diplodocidae family. It had a small head on an extra-long neck and thick legs with five-toed feet to support its weight. Its name is pronounced di-plod-oh-cus.

NAME: DIPLODOCUS

LIVED: NORTH AMERICA

DIET: HERBIVORE

LENGTH: 105 FT (32 M)

WEIGHT: 35,300 LB (16,000 KG)

STRUTHIOMIMUS

A Late Cretaceous Period dinosaur, Struthiomimus was a theropod, part of the saurischian group. It was in the Ornithomimidae family of ostrich-like dinosaurs. It had a toothless horny beak, powerful claws on its arms, and long, slim back legs, which would have made it a fast runner. Its name is pronounced strooth-ee-oh-mime-us.

NAME: STRUTHIOMIMUS

LIVED: NORTH AMERICA

DIET: OMNIVORE

LENGTH: 14 FT (4.3 M)

WEIGHT: 330 LB (150 KG)

SARCOSUCHUS

Sarchosuchus was not a dinosaur: it was a swimming reptile that lived in Africa and South America during the Cretaceous Period, about 112 million years ago. It was a member of the Pholidosauridae family of crocodile-like reptiles, closely related to today's crocodiles, alligators, and caimans. Its name is pronounced sar-ko-sook-us.

NAME: SARCOSUCHUS

LIVED: SOUTH AMERICA AND AFRICA

DIET: CARNIVORE

LENGTH: 39 FT (12 M)

WEIGHT: 17,600 LB (8,000 KG)

ARCHAEOPTERYX

Archaeopteryx was a saurischian birdlike creature that is often named as one of the earliest known birds. It lived around 150 million years ago in the Late Jurassic Period, in what is now Germany. It grew up to 1 foot 6 inches (0.5 m) long, about the size of a modern raven. Its name is pronounced ar-kee-op-ter-ix.

NAME: ARCHAEOPTERYX

LIVED: EUROPE

DIET: CARNIVORE

LENGTH: 1.5 FT (0.5 M)

WEIGHT: 2.2 LB (1 KG)

PTERANODON

The Pteranodon was a flying reptile that lived during the Late Cretaceous Period. It was not a dinosaur, though it was a close relative. Its wingspan was longer than any known bird today at 35 feet (10.5 m), and it is thought that its long head crest helped to balance it out because of its long beak. Its name is pronounced tear-ann-owe-don.

NAME: PTERANODON

LIVED: NORTH AMERICA AND EUROPE

DIET: CARNIVORE

WINGSPAN: 35 FT (10.5 M)

WEIGHT: UP TO 205 LB (93 KG)

BRONTOSAURUS

Brontosaurus was a plant-eating sauropod in the saurischian group of dinosaurs. It lived in North America in the Late Jurassic Period. It was in the Diplodocidae family, which includes some of the largest animals ever to walk the Earth. Compared to the brachiosaurus, the diplodocids were quite slender but extremely long. Brontosaurus reached 65 feet (20 m) long. Its name is pronounced bront-oh-saw-rus.

NAME: BRONTOSAURUS

LIVED: NORTH AMERICA

DIET: HERBIVORE

LENGTH: 65 FT (20 M)

WEIGHT: 33,600 LB (15,250 KG)

MEGANEURA

PIECES REQUIRED

2x   1x   1x   1x   2x   1x   2x

1x   3x   1x   2x   1x   2x

4x   If you want to make your Meganeura look more realistic, you can always use transparent bricks to make the wings instead of the white 4x1 bricks.

1   1x   1x

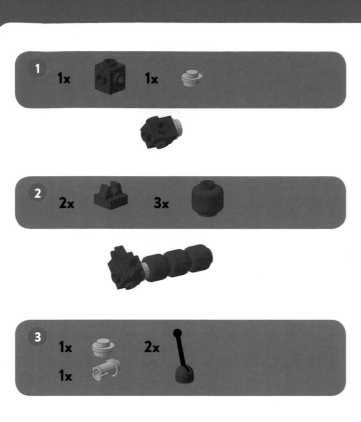

2   2x   3x

3   1x   2x   1x

4   1x   1x   2x

5   1x   1x   1x   1x

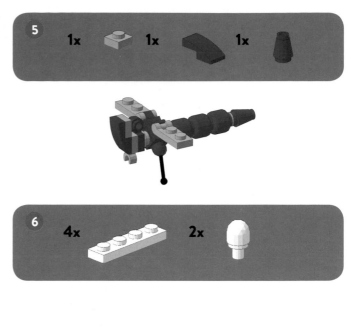

6   4x   2x

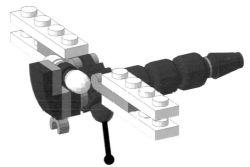

FACT

- The first Meganeura was discovered in France in 1880 and named by French paleontologist Charles Brongniart in 1885.

- Their diets were mostly made up of other insects and small amphibians.

- The Meganeura are part of an extinct order called Meganisoptera, or Griffinflies.

TRILOBITE

PIECES REQUIRED

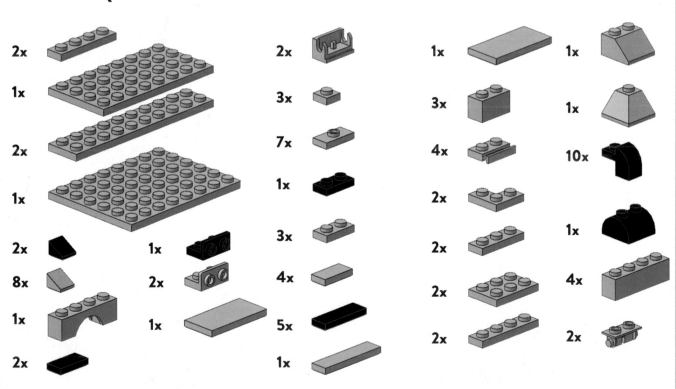

2x
1x
2x
1x
2x
8x
1x
2x

1x
2x
1x

2x
3x
7x
1x
3x
4x
5x
1x

1x
3x
4x
2x
2x
2x

1x
1x
10x
1x
4x
2x

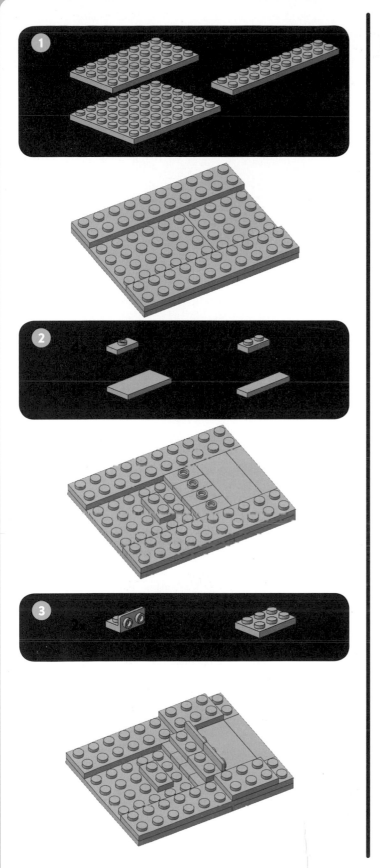

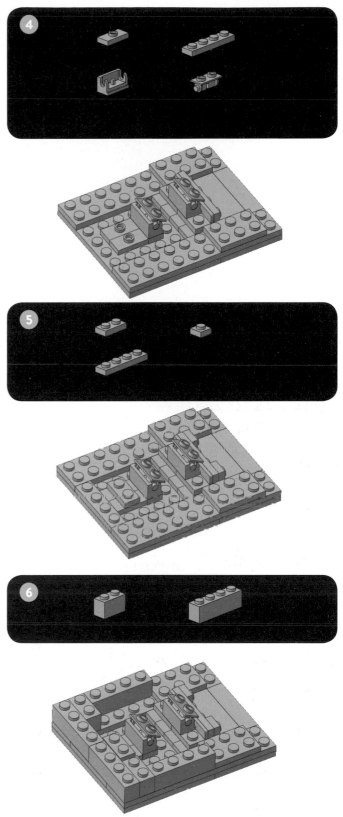

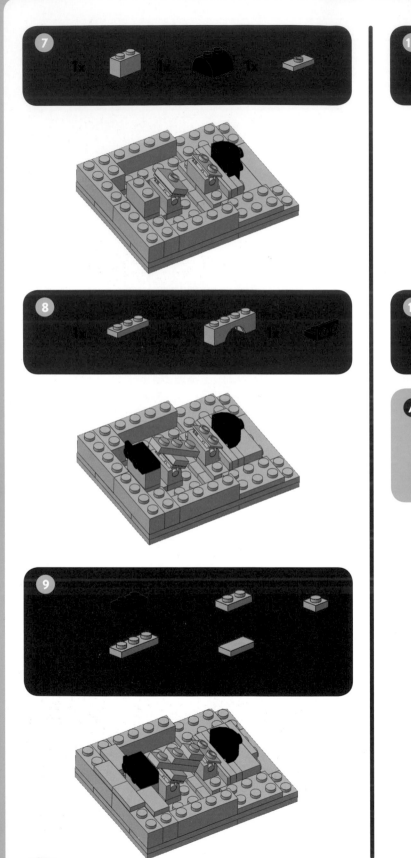

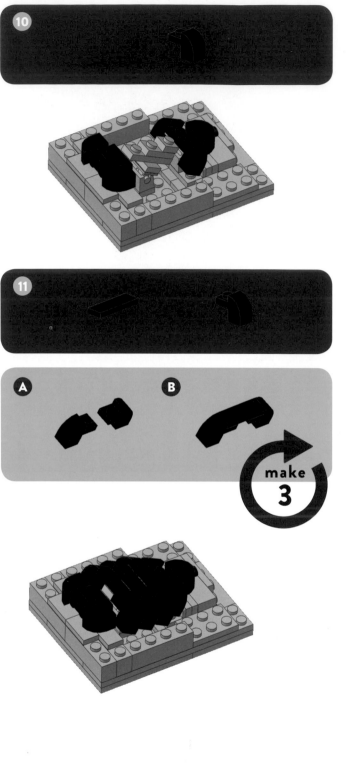

make
3

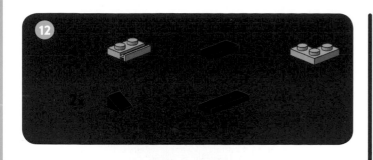

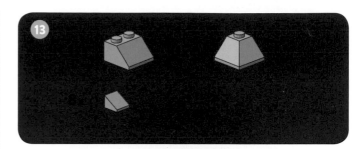

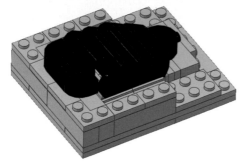

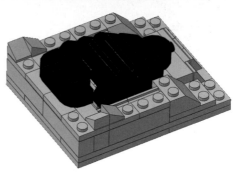

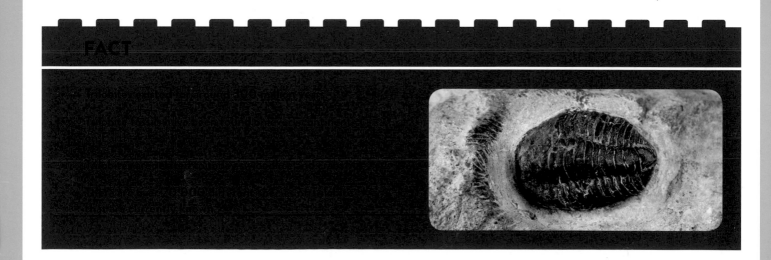

LIVING ON THE LAND

During the 160 million or so years that dinosaurs ruled the land, the Earth was changing. Many new species of dinosaurs evolved and died out as these amazing reptiles adapted to changing climates and habitats.

HABITATS

For most of the Triassic Period, all the Earth's dry land was joined together into one continent that earth scientists have named Pangaea. This meant that animals and plants could spread easily across the entire world. The climate was hot and dry, with no ice at either pole. Much of Pangaea's interior was desert. By the Late Triassic Period, when dinosaurs emerged, the continents had started to drift apart, caused by movements of the great plates of rock that make up the Earth's outer crust.

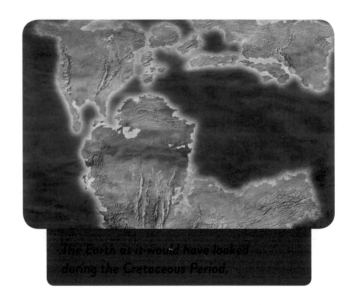

The Earth as it would have looked during the Cretaceous Period.

During the Jurassic Period, the climate was much wetter. Deserts were replaced by rain forests. Dinosaurs were the major land-living vertebrates, but they were accompanied by other reptiles, amphibians, and mammals. Insects and flying reptiles, such as pterosaurs, were in the skies. In the seas and rivers, the largest creatures were fish and marine reptiles, including turtles, crocodiles, and plesiosaurs. At this time, the continents were splitting, and seas were reaching previously dry areas.

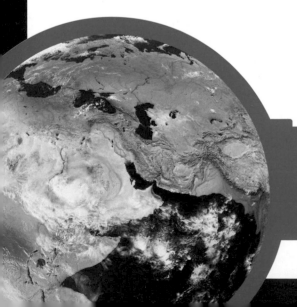

Around 250 million years ago, all of the continents on Earth were part of one big supercontinent named Pangaea. It was surrounded by one big super-ocean, called Panthalassa.

The planet cooled during the following Cretaceous Period, and the climate became more varied. There were icy mountains and poles and warmer deserts, forests, and grasslands. Groups of dinosaurs evolved different characteristics to help them find food in their different habitats. For example, fish-eating dinosaurs such as Spinosaurus lived in the swamps of what would become North Africa. It had crocodile-like jaws perfect for snapping up fish. The continents were now separate landmasses, each of them with their different suites of animals.

BEHAVIOR

All dinosaurs lived on land, even though people sometimes mistakenly say that flying reptiles like Pterodactylus, and swimming reptiles like Sarcosuchus, were dinosaurs. During the Jurassic Period, some meat-eating dinosaurs developed feathers and evolved into birds. At the point when a dinosaur species was able to fly properly, paleontologists call them birds rather than dinosaurs. Not everyone agrees on whether creatures such as Archaeopteryx, which had wings but could probably only make short, gliding flights, should be called an early bird or a birdlike dinosaur.

When they try to work out how dinosaurs behaved, paleontologists turn to their closest living relatives, the birds and crocodiles, for clues. Like birds and crocodiles, dinosaurs laid eggs in nests. Birds and crocodiles often live together in groups. Paleontologists think some dinosaurs behaved the same way. They may have lived in herds, which was helpful for protecting their young, finding a mate, and defense against predators. Birds communicate with each other through calls, as well as displays such as strutting and spreading their tails. Crocodiles communicate through hisses, chirps, and bellows. Scientists think that dinosaurs also communicated with each other through displays, and perhaps through calls.

Plants that were around during the time of the dinosaurs that we still see today include ferns, yews, redwoods, and the Araucaria Araucana, or monkey-puzzle tree (above).

DINOSAUR EGG

PIECES REQUIRED

3x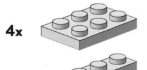

4x

4x

4x

8x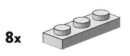

9x

8x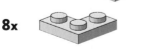

3x

8x

6x

2x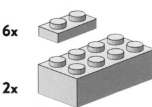

1 2x 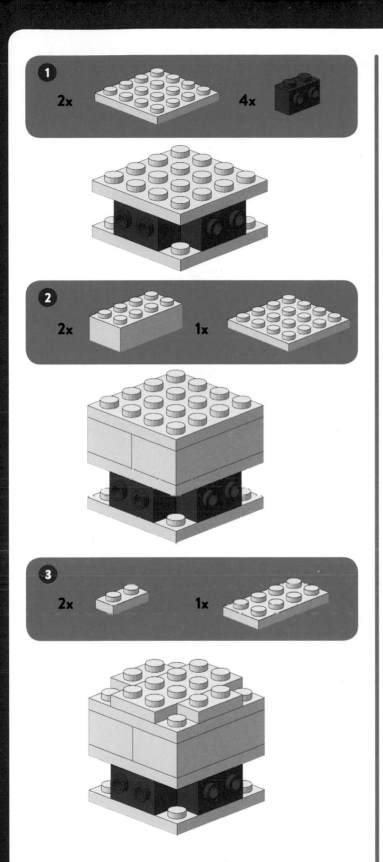 4x

2 2x 1x

3 2x 1x

4 2x 1x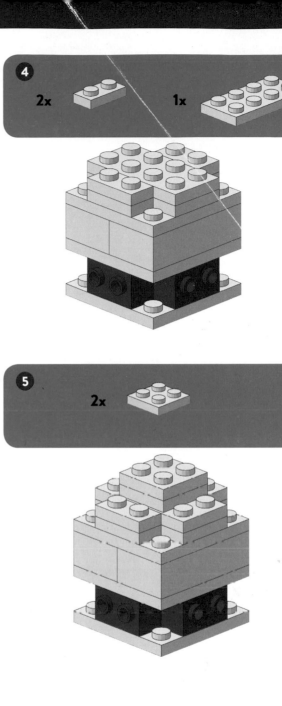

5 2x

6

2x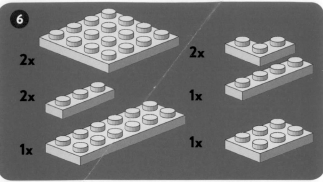
2x
1x

2x
1x
1x

A

B

C

make

4

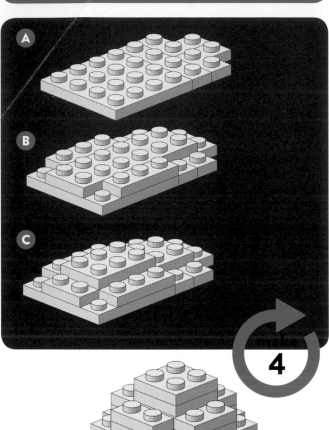

7

4x 1x

8

1x

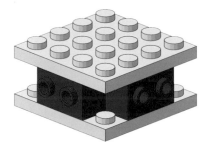

9

1x 2x
1x

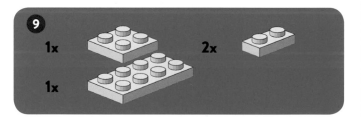

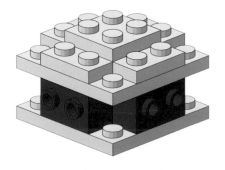

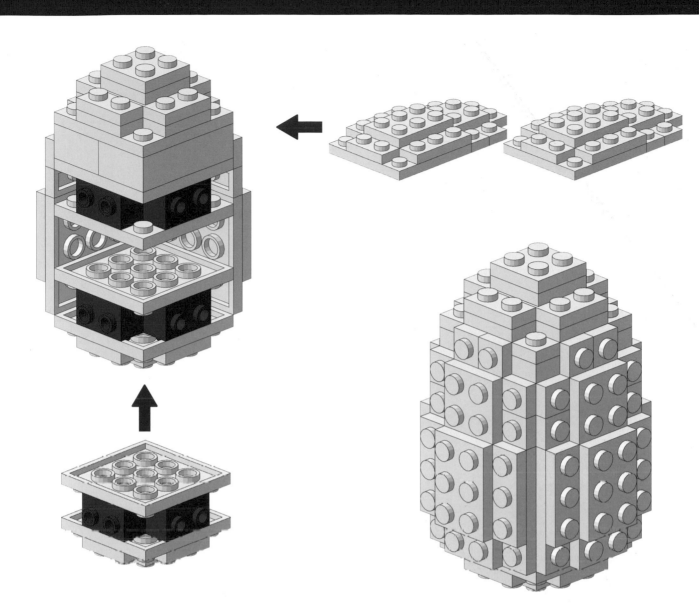

PARASAUROLOPHUS

PIECES REQUIRED

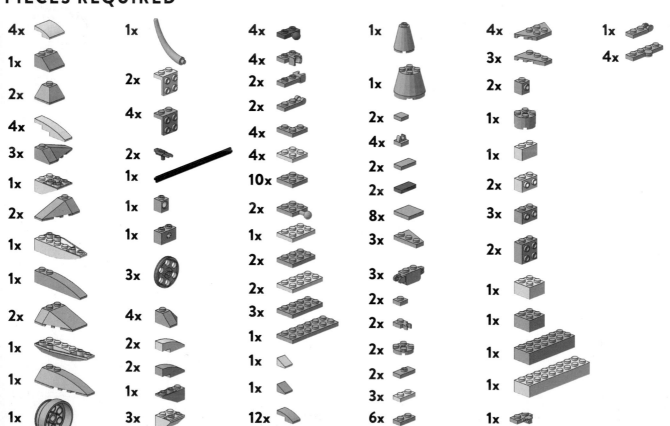

4x		1x		4x		1x		4x	
1x				4x				3x	
2x		2x		2x		1x		2x	
4x		4x		2x		2x		1x	
3x				4x		4x		1x	
1x		2x		4x		2x		2x	
2x		1x		10x		2x		3x	
1x		1x		2x		8x		2x	
1x		1x		1x		3x		1x	
2x		3x		2x		3x		1x	
1x		4x		2x		2x		1x	
1x		2x		3x		2x			
1x		2x		1x		2x			
		1x		1x		3x			
		3x		12x		6x		1x	

40

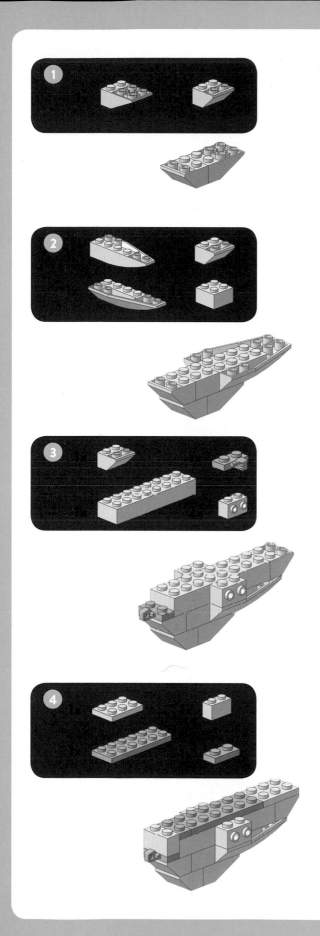

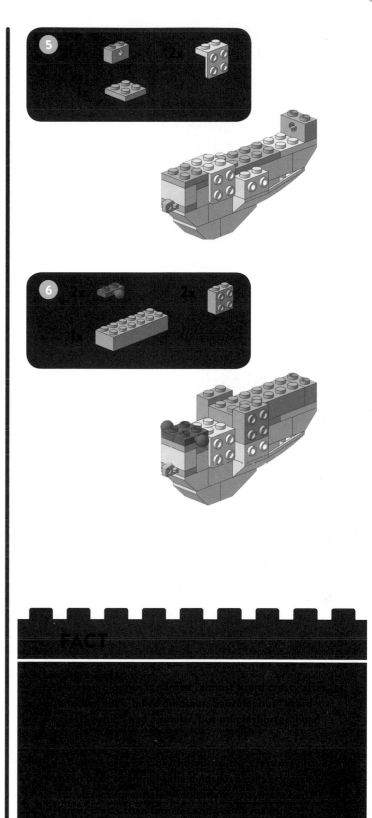

FACT

7
1x 1x
1x 1x

8
2x 1x
1x 2x

9
1x 4x
1x 1x

10
1x 1x
1x 1x

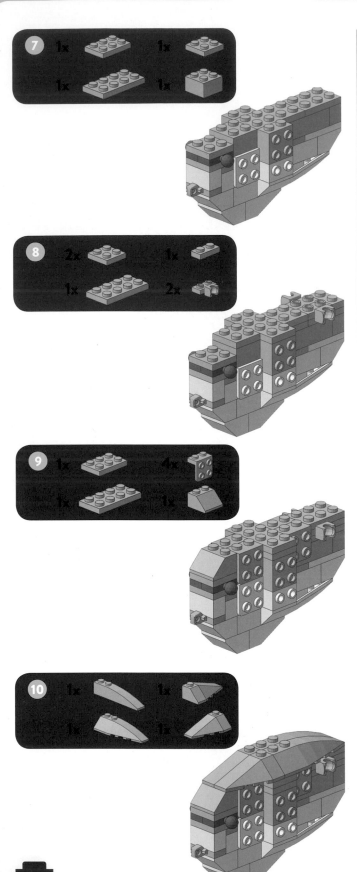

11
1x 1x
1x 2x

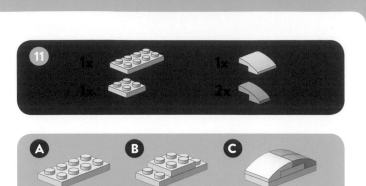

A B C

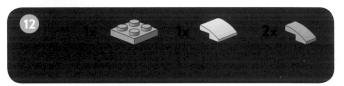

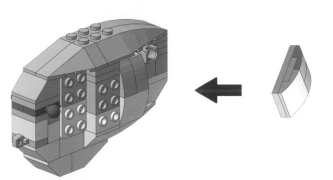

12
1x 1x 2x

A B

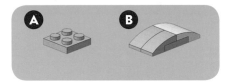

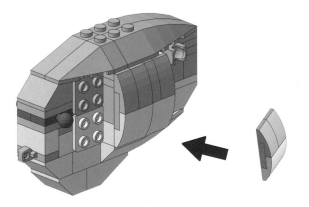

13

A

B

C

D

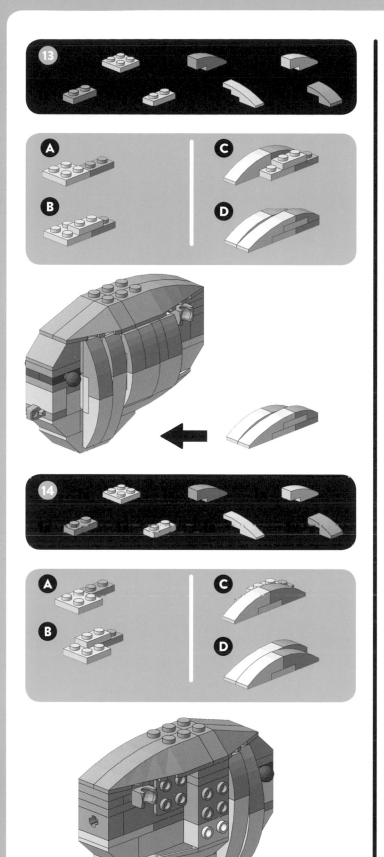

14

A

B

C

D

15

A

B

16

1x

2x

A

B

C

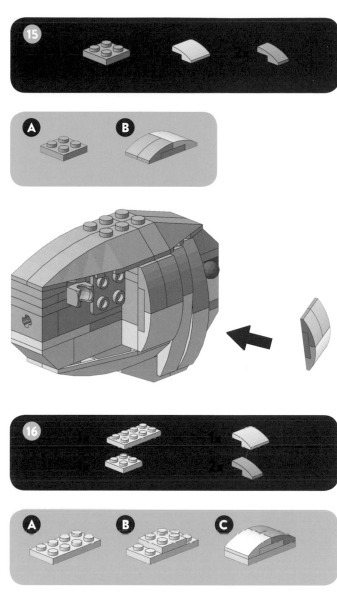

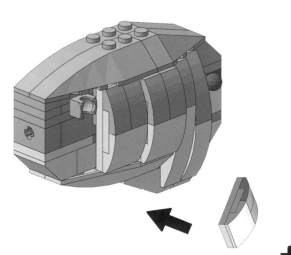

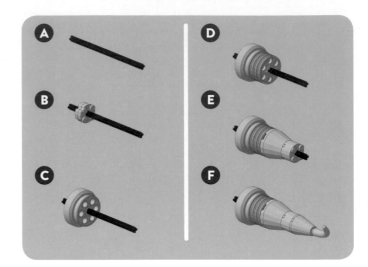

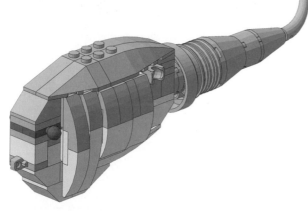

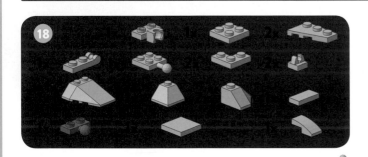

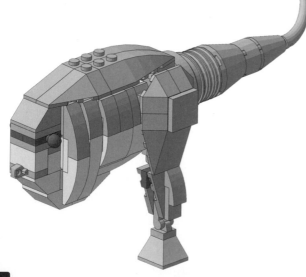

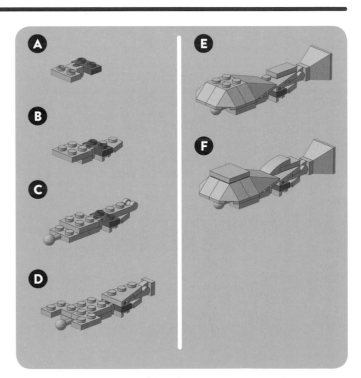

19

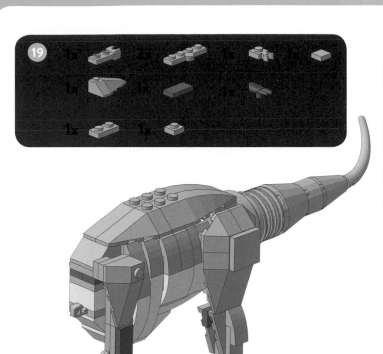

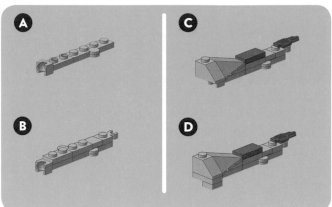

A

B

C

D

20

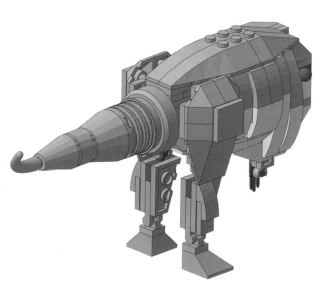

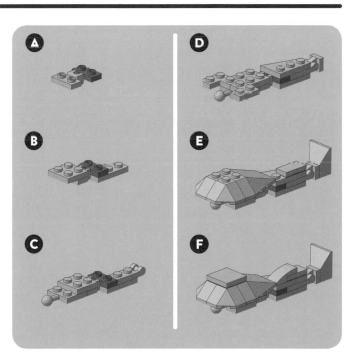

A

B

C

D

E

F

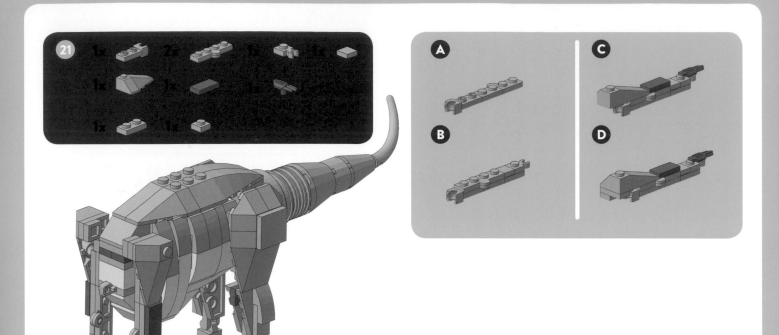

21

1x 2x 1x 1x
1x 1x 1x
1x 1x

A

B

C

D

22

3x 1x 2x

A

B

C

D

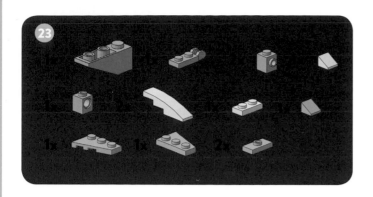

23

1x 1x 1x
1x
1x 1x 2x

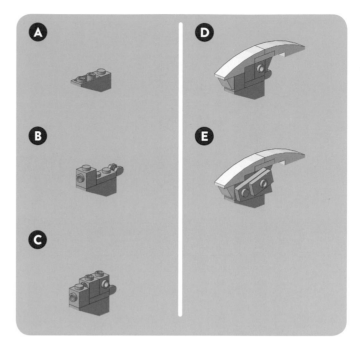

A

B

C

D

E

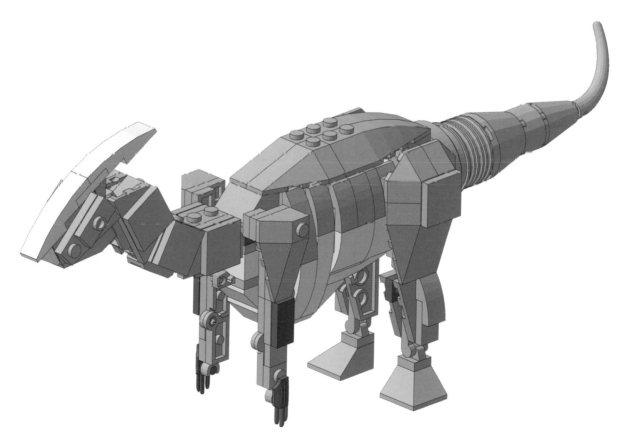

PARASAUROLOPHUS

The Parasaurolophus was an herbivore and would have eaten mostly pine needles, leaves, and twigs.

CORYTHOSAURUS

PIECES REQUIRED

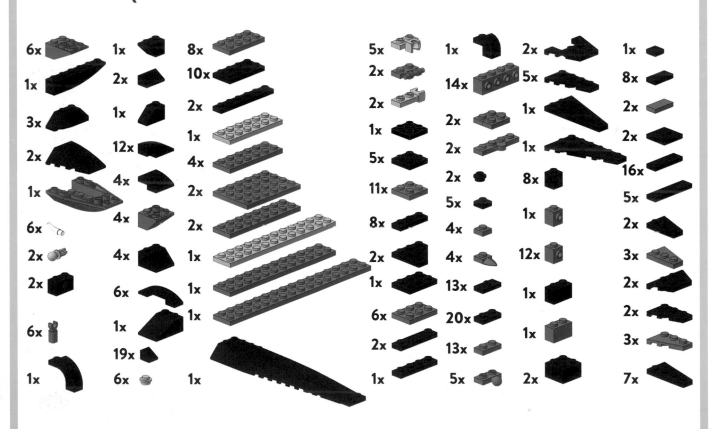

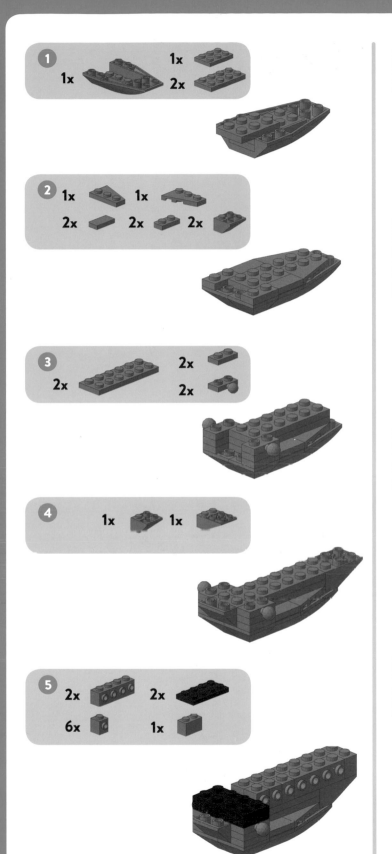

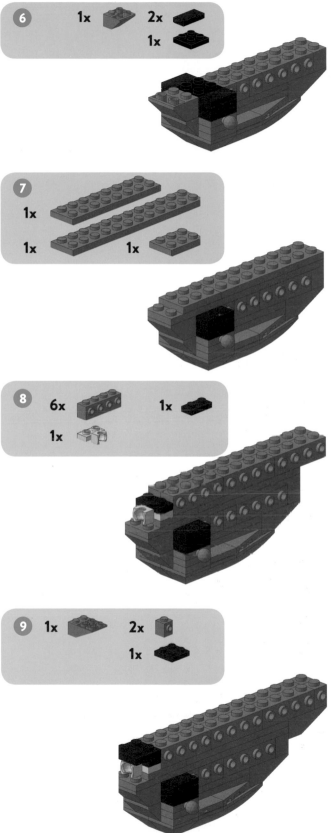

10
2x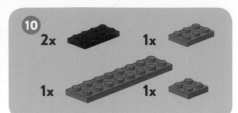
1x

1x
1x

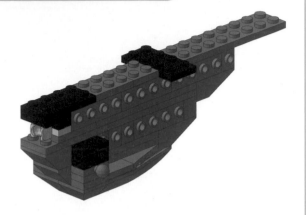

11
1x
1x

1x
1x

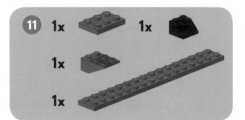

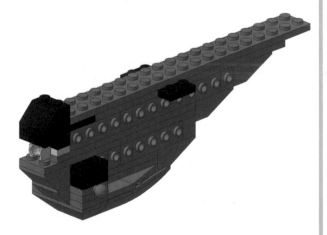

12
3x
1x
2x

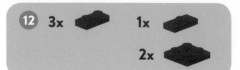

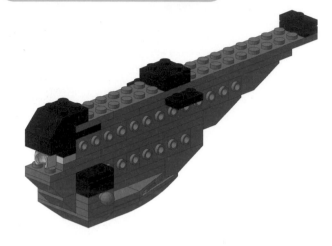

13
6x
2x
2x
4x

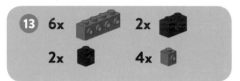

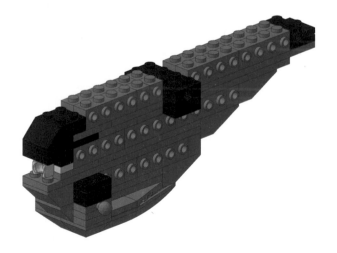

14 1x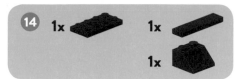

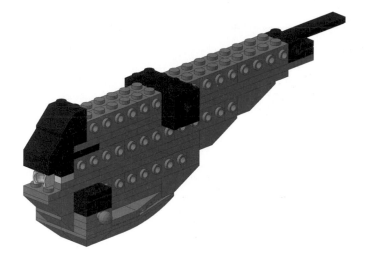

15 1x

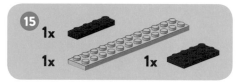

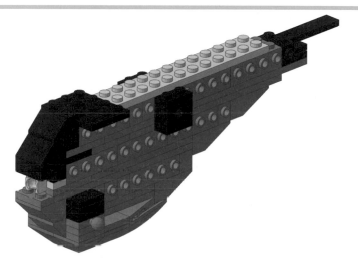

16 1x 2x

1x

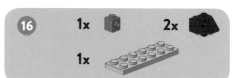

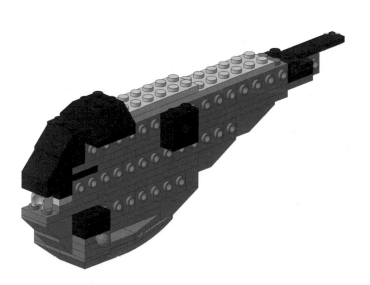

17
1x
1x
1x

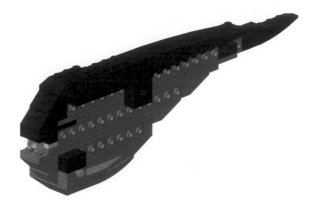

18
2x
8x

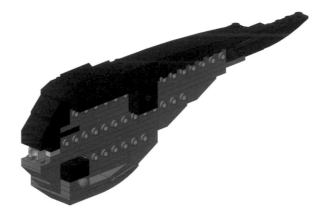

19
3x   1x
2x   3x
1x   3x
6x   3x
4x   2x
2x   3x
1x   1x
1x   1x
1x   2x
1x   6x
1x   1x
2x   1x
1x   1x

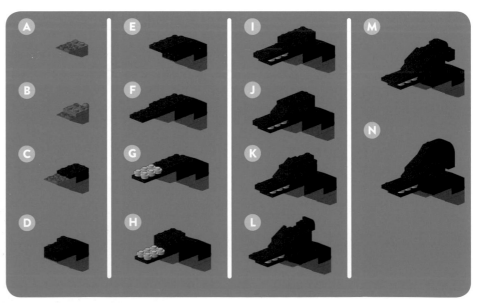

A   E   I   M
B   F   J
C   G   K   N
D   H   L

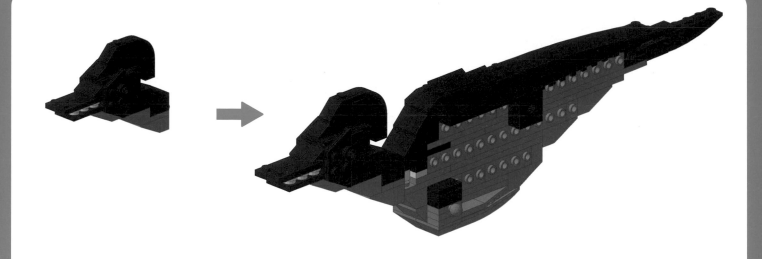

20

3x 1x 1x
1x 1x 2x

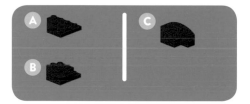
A
B C

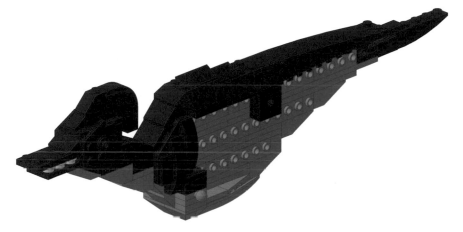

21

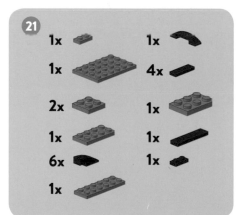
1x 1x
1x 4x
2x 1x
1x 1x
6x 1x
1x

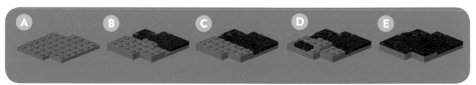
A B C D E

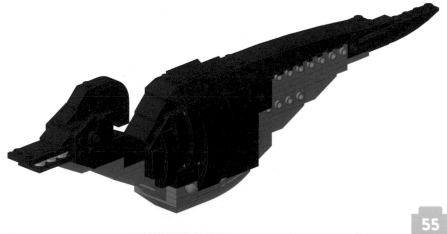

22

1x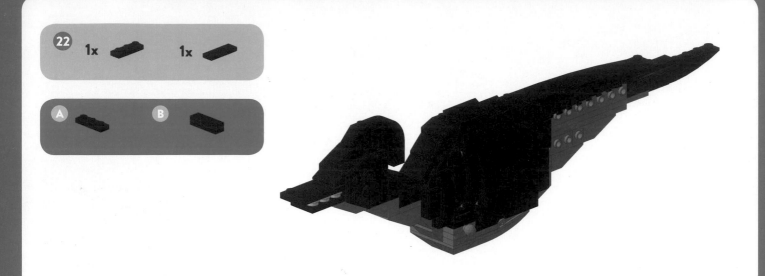

1x

A   **B**

23

1x 1x 1x 1x 1x 1x 2x 2x 1x

3x 1x 1x 1x

PART 1

A   **B**   **C**

PART 2

A   **C**

B   **D**

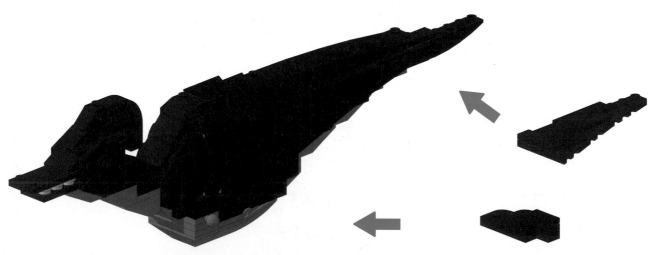

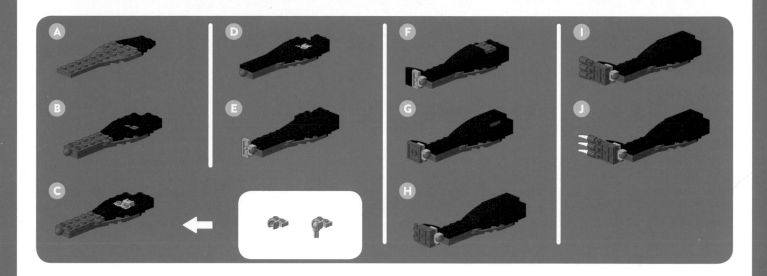

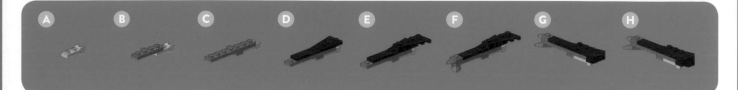

25 1x 1x 1x 2x 1x 1x 1x 2x 1x 1x

A   B   C   D   E   F   G   H

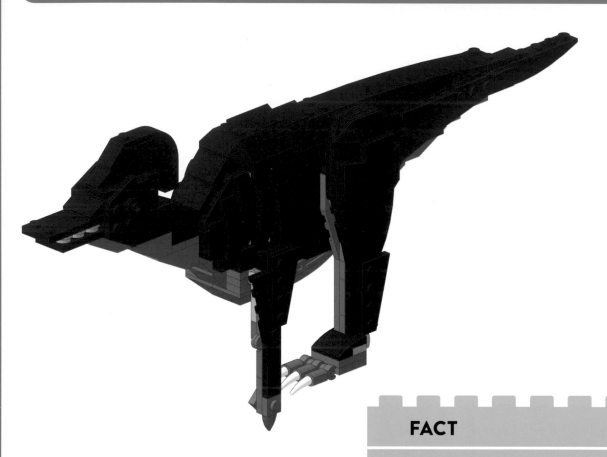

FACT

- Corythosaurus's name means "helmet lizard." Its fan-shaped head crest was about 1 foot (30 cm) high. Hollow passages, through which Corythosaurus breathed, ran up into the crest and back down through its snout. These hollow tubes and chambers would have amplified Corythosaurus's calls, rather like a trombone.

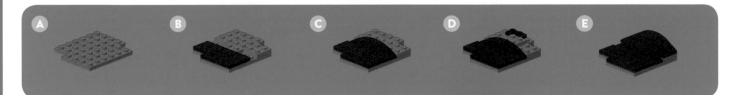

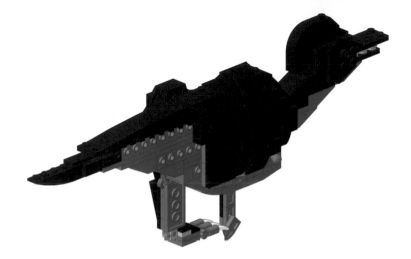

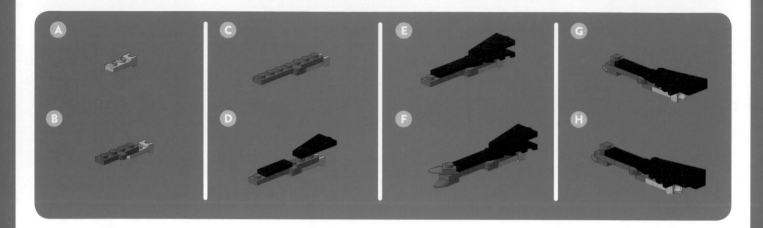

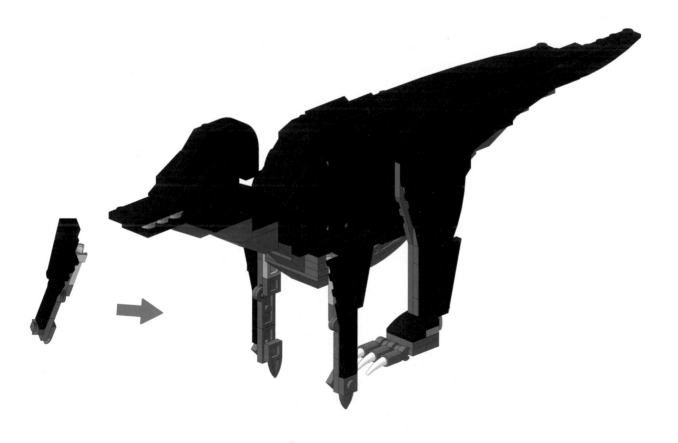

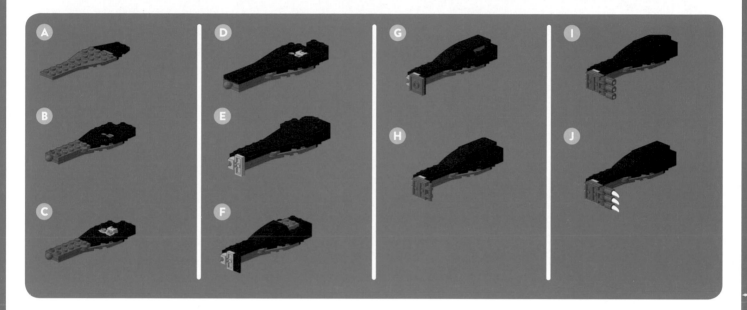

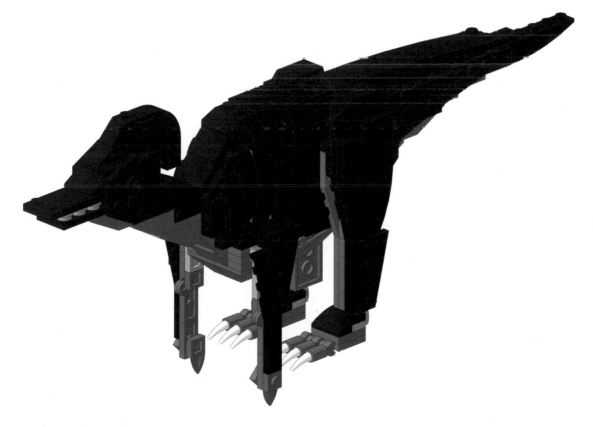

CORYTHOSAURUS

The first specimen of Corythosaurus found was almost a complete specimen—it even had fossilized skin! Unfortunately, the entire specimen was lost at sea when the ship carrying it to Britain sunk during the World War I.

ATTACK AND DEFENSE

Like animals alive today, dinosaurs evolved many methods of attacking their prey and defending themselves from predators. Some methods made use of physical features, such as sharp teeth or body armor. Other methods were behaviors, such as herding together for safety.

ATTACK

Meat-eating dinosaurs had big, sharp teeth and strong jaws for killing their prey. If they attacked like modern meat-eating animals, they probably aimed their bites at the soft neck or belly, where an injury could do most damage. Meat-eaters also had claws, which were used to slash at, and grab hold of, prey. The Dromaeosauridae family of dinosaurs had an especially long curved claw on the second toe of each foot, which may have been used to

The Euoplocephalus had an armored body, and a spiked club at its tail.

climb up large prey as well as to stab and to rip out stomachs.

Like many predators today, some meat-eaters probably had excellent eyesight and sense of smell, which allowed them to locate prey at a distance. For some meat-eaters, such as Tyrannosaurus, their great size must have been an advantage. Tyrannosaurus was around 40 feet (12 m) long. It may have barrelled into prey with great force, sending even a large Triceratops flying. Some smaller meat-eaters were extremely

The Deinonychus had a 5 inch (13 cm) long razor-sharp claw on each rear foot. It could rotate quickly through 180 degrees and was used to slash at and hang onto prey.

Adult dinosaurs may have formed a protective ring around their young when threatened.

fast runners: Dromaeosaurus could chase down prey at speeds of at least 20 miles per hour. It had long legs and light bones.

DEFENSE

Some plant-eaters, including the ankylosaurs, like Aletopelta, had their back, sides, and tail covered in flat plates of bone, which acted as armor to protect them from bites and slashes. It is possible that these dinosaurs lay down when attacked, so they could not be flipped over to reveal their softer undersides. The long tails of many plant-eaters could have delivered a hard blow. Some paleontologists think that the extra-long tails of some sauropods, such as Diplodocus, could be lashed like a whip. Some plant-eaters, such as Euoplocephalus, had bony clubs at the end of their tail, while others, such as Stegosaurus, had spikes.

Plant-eaters probably had good hearing so they could get early warning of an approaching predator. It is believed that Parasaurolophus could make a loud honking noise, amplified by the hollow crest on its head, to warn other members of its herd. A herd of horned dinosaurs, such as Triceratops, may have turned their horns outward on attackers.

The largest plant-eaters, such as Giraffatitan, which was three stories high, would have been immune to attack from all but the very biggest meat-eaters. Ornithomimids were probably the fastest plant-eaters as well as the fastest dinosaurs of all. These ostrich-like dinosaurs could outrun their predators at up to 40 miles (65 km) per hour.

TRICERATOPS

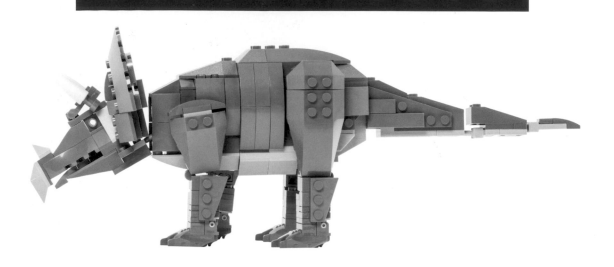

PIECES REQUIRED

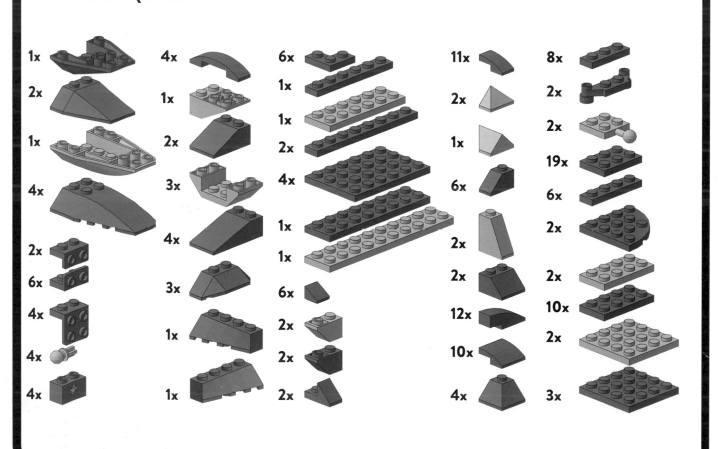

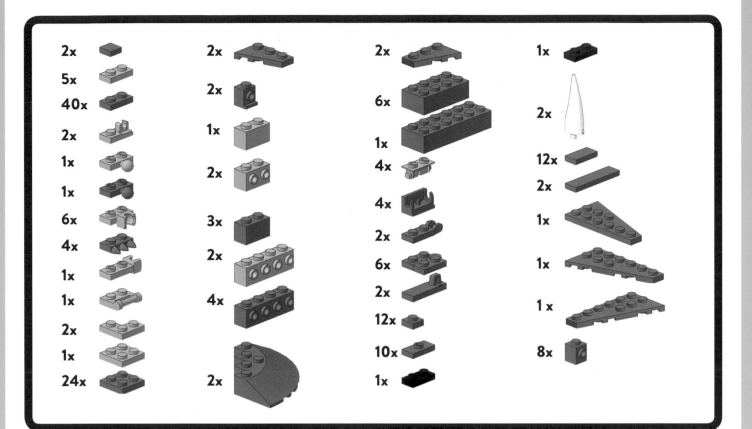

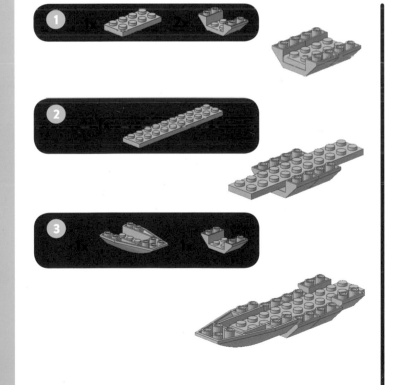

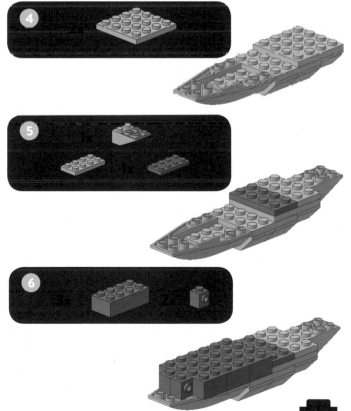

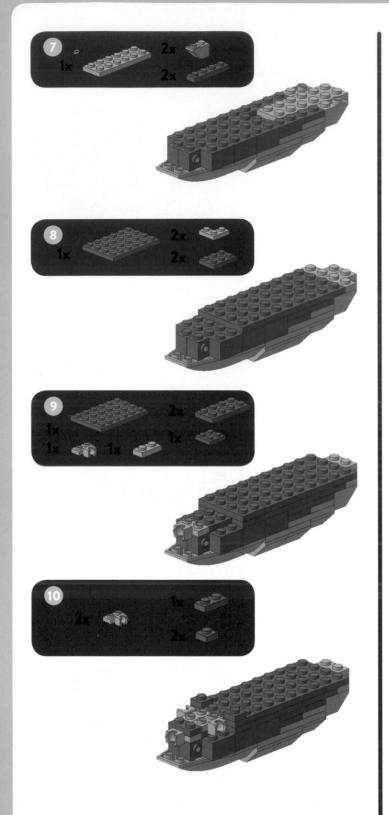

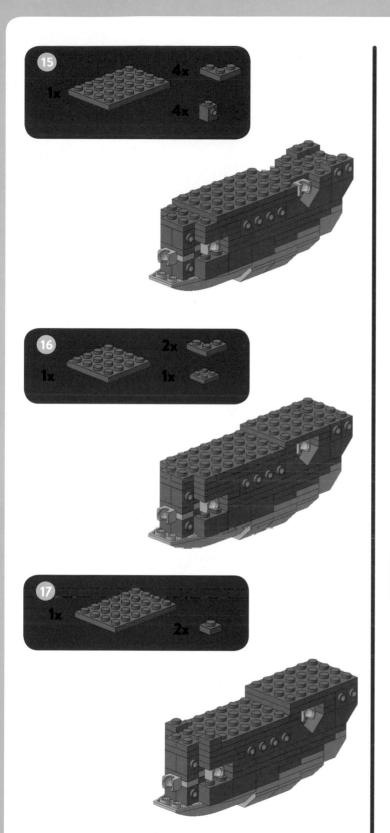
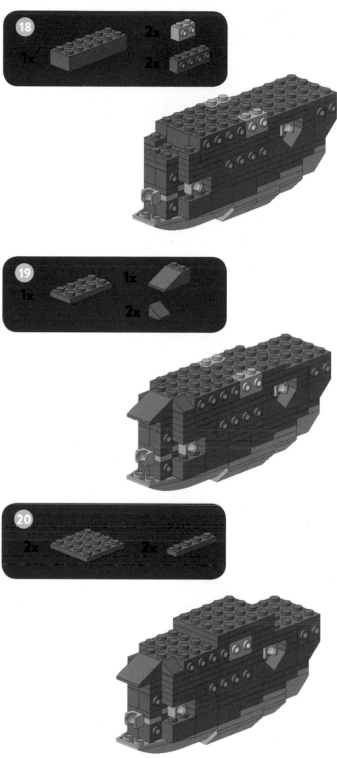

21

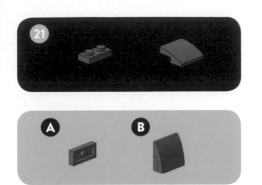

A B

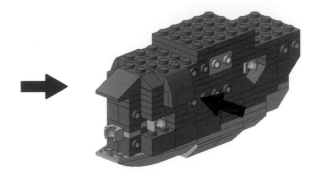

22

A B

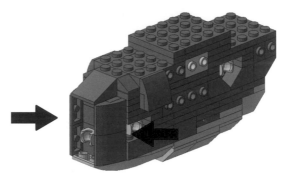

23

24

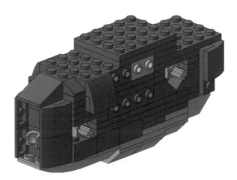

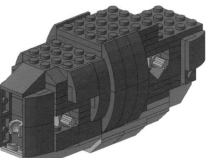

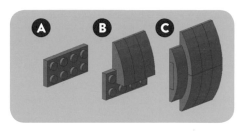

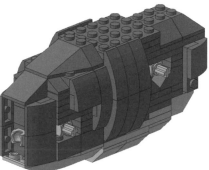

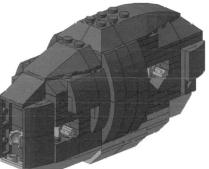

FACT

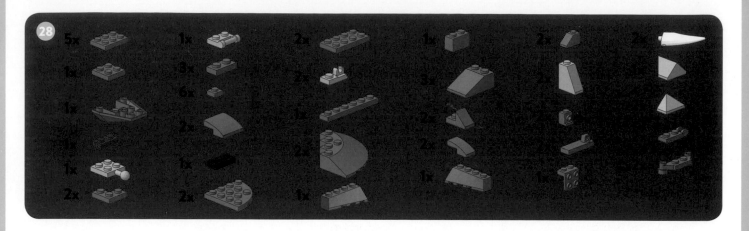

PART 1

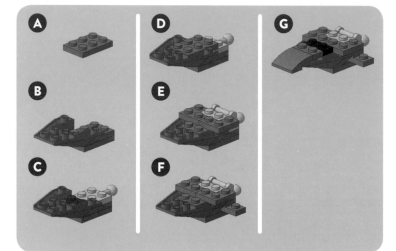

PART 2

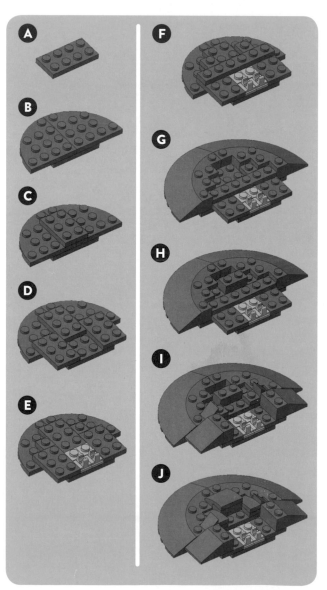

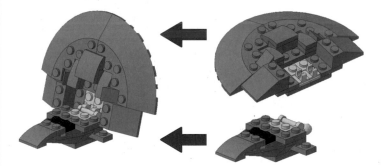

PART 3

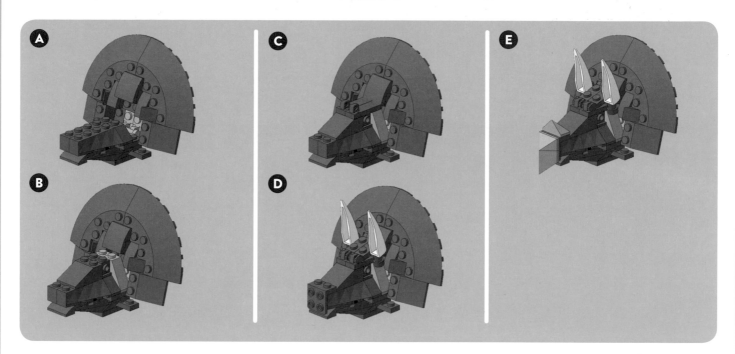

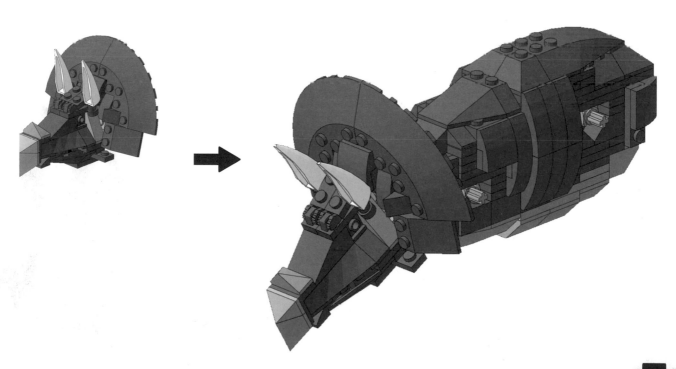

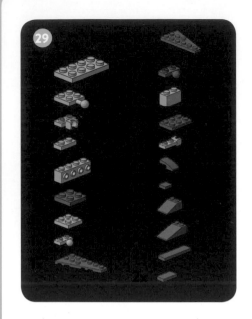

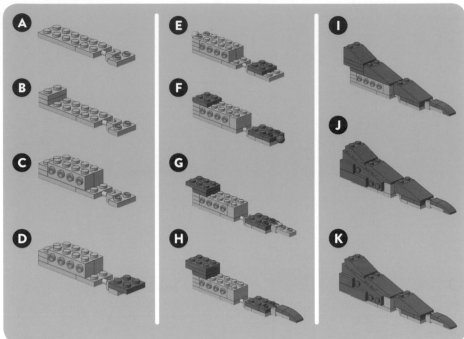

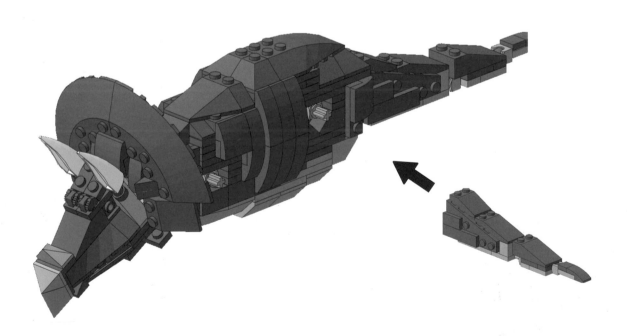

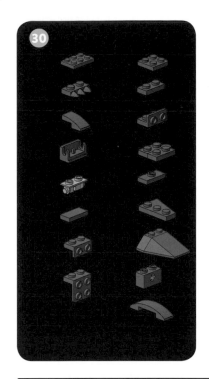

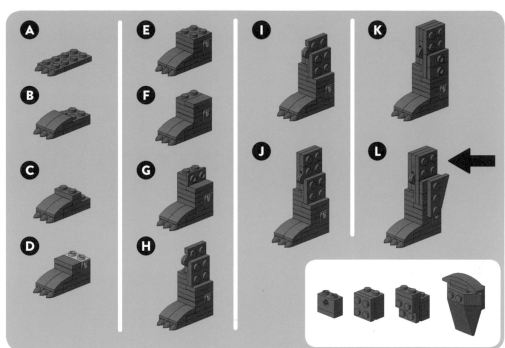

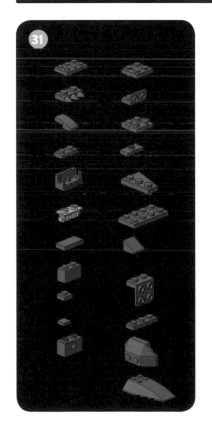

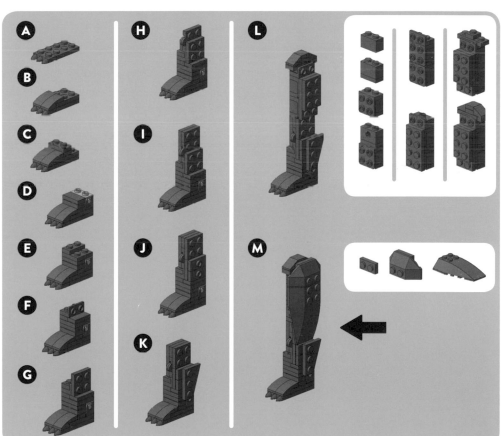

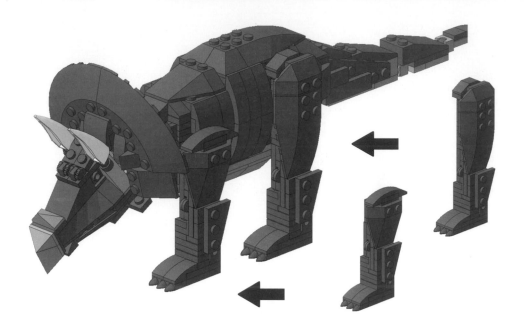

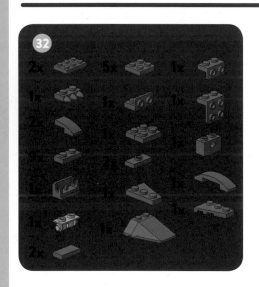

32

2x 5x 1x
1x 1x 1x
2x
9x 2x
1x 1x
1x 1x
1x 1x
2x

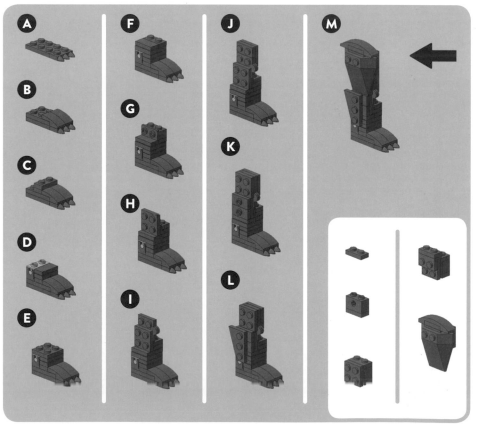

A

B

C

D

E

F

G

H

I

J

K

L

M

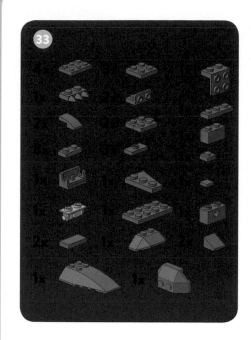

33

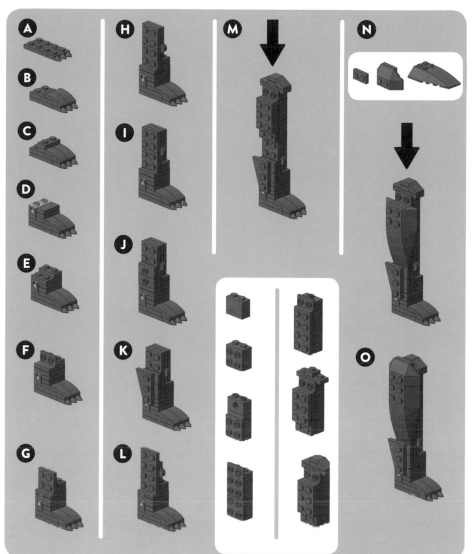

A B C D E F G H I J K L M N O

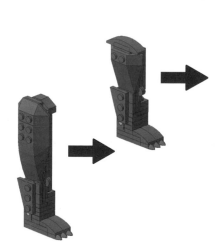

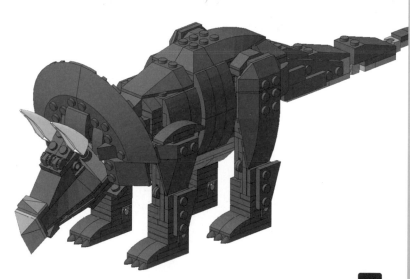

TRICERATOPS
Triceratops was named for the ancient Greek for "three-horned face." Triceratop's horns and neck frill may have been used for defense, but paleontologists believe they were mostly used for display. Today's male horned or antlered creatures often use them in combat with other males of their species and to attract females.

ALETOPELTA

PIECES REQUIRED

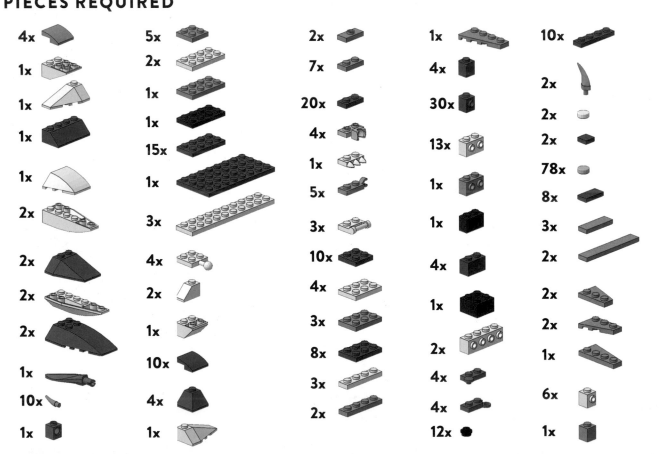

4x	5x	2x	1x	10x
1x	2x	7x	4x	2x
1x	1x	20x	30x	2x
1x	1x	4x	13x	2x
1x	15x	1x	1x	78x
2x	1x	5x	1x	8x
2x	3x	3x	4x	3x
2x	4x	10x	1x	2x
2x	2x	4x	2x	2x
2x	1x	3x	4x	2x
1x	10x	8x	4x	1x
10x	4x	3x	12x	6x
1x	1x	2x		1x

1

2x

2

1x

3

1x 2x

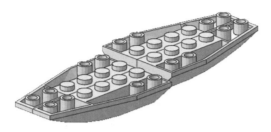

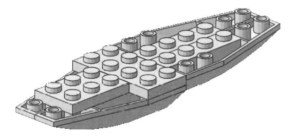

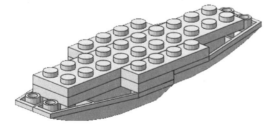

4

1x 1x

1x

5

2x 1x 1x

6

4x 8x 4x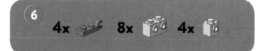

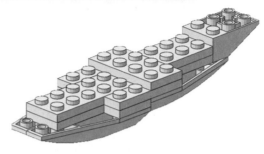

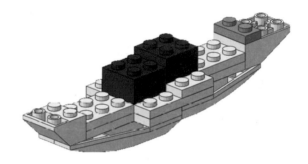

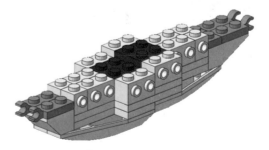

7

1x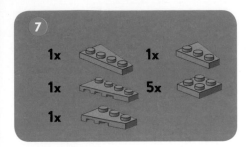
1x
1x
1x
5x

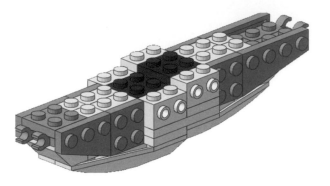

8

2x
2x
4x

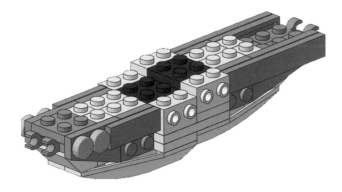

9

2x
1x
1x
1x
1x

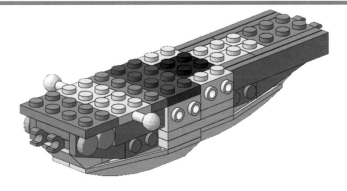

10

2x
1x
1x
1x

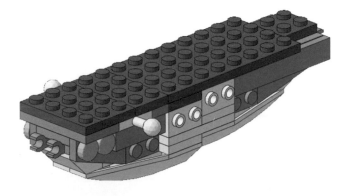

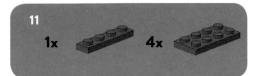

11

1x   4x

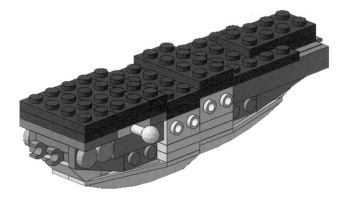

12

2x

4x   1x

18x   1x

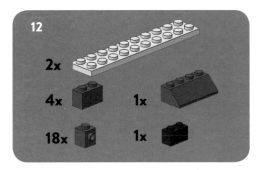

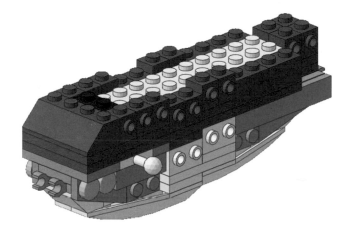

FACT

- An Aletopelta's body armour was made of knobs and plates of bone that were not attached to its skeleton but formed part of its skin (except for the head, where the plates were fused to the skull).

- The plates ranged from 1 cm (0.4 in) to 35 cm (14 in) in length, and were differently shaped depending on the body part they covered, to allow the dinosaur to move freely.

13

1x 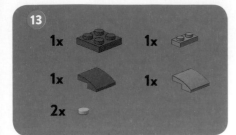 1x

1x 1x

2x

 A B

 A B

make
4

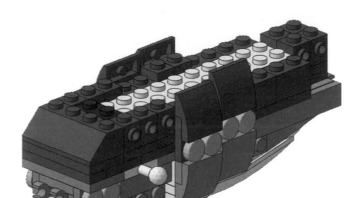

14

2x 1x

2x

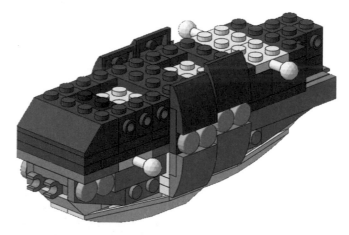

15

4x  1x

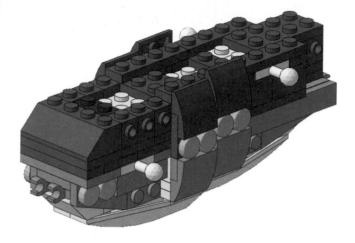

16

2x 1x

2x

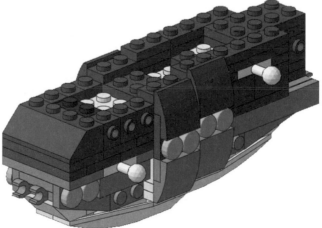

17

1x  1x

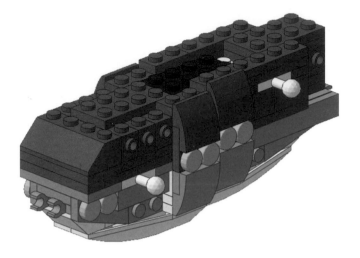

18

2x

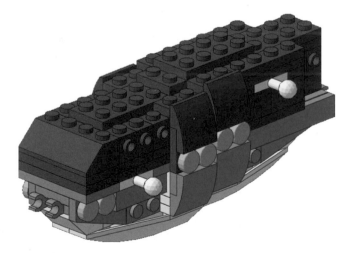

19 2x 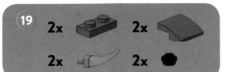 2x

A **B**

A **B**

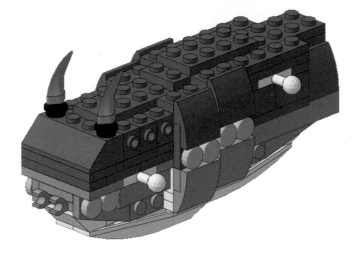

20

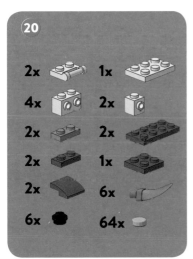

A **B** **C** **D** **E** **F** **G** **H**

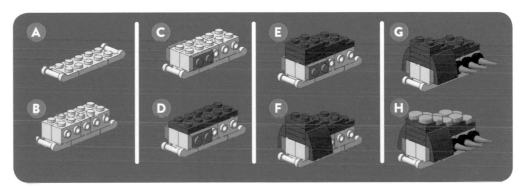

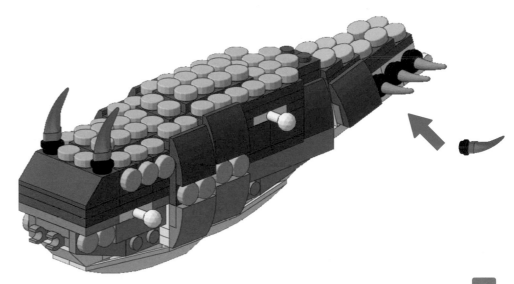

21

1x 1x

1x 1x

4x

1x 4x

1x 4x

A B C D E F

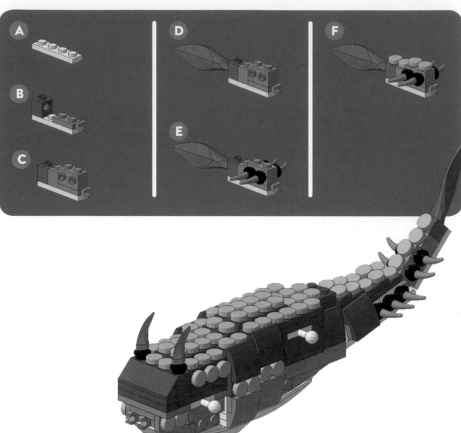

22

1x 2x 1x 1x 2x 1x 2x 1x

1x 1x 1x 1x 4x 1x 1x 2x 4x 2x

A B C D E F G H I

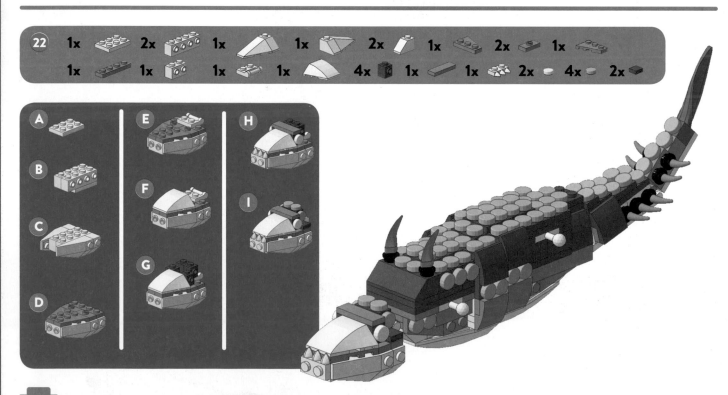

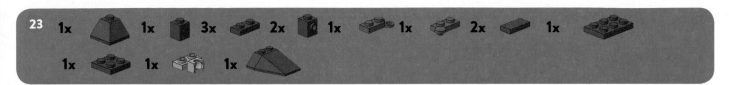

23 1x 1x 3x 2x 1x 1x 2x 1x

1x 1x 1x

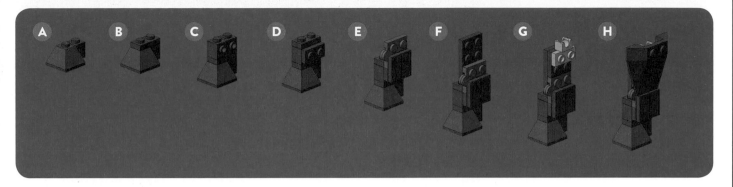

A B C D E F G H

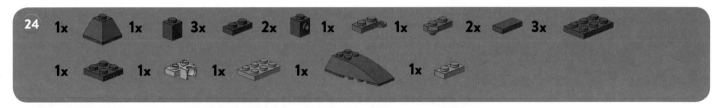

24 1x 1x 3x 2x 1x 1x 2x 3x

1x 1x 1x 1x 1x

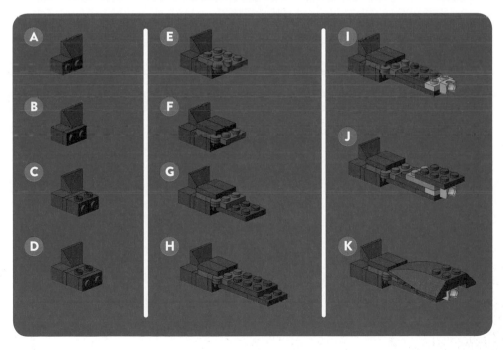

A E I

B F J

C G

D H K

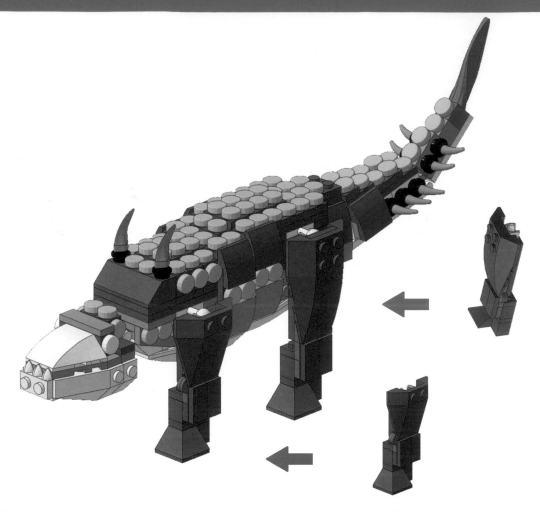

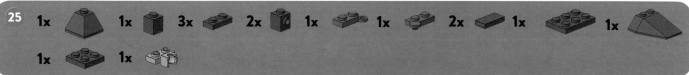

25   1x   1x   3x   2x   1x   1x   2x   1x   1x

1x   1x

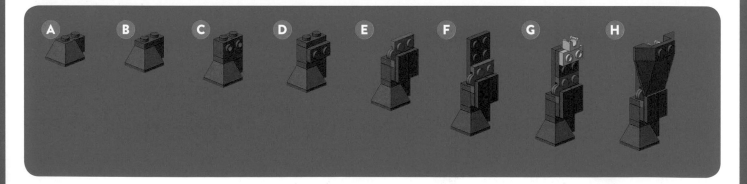

A   B   C   D   E   F   G   H

26

1x 1x 2x 2x 1x 1x 2x 3x

1x 1x 1x 1x 1x

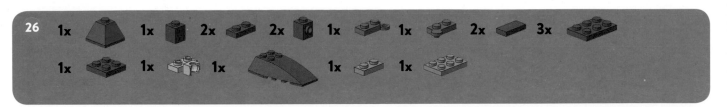

A B C D E F G H I J K

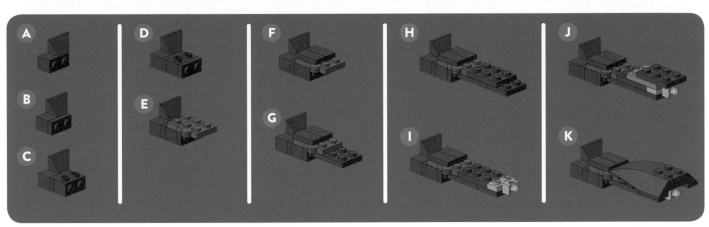

27

1x 1x

A B

make
4

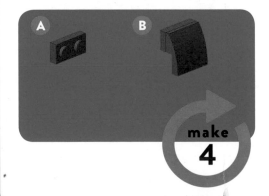

ALETOPELTA

The Aletopelta is part of a group of dinosaurs called ankylosaurs. The fossilized remains of the Aletopelta were found near the Californian coast. It is thought that after it died, the Aletopelta's body floated out to sea and became a small reef-like environment for the sea life.

STEGOSAURUS

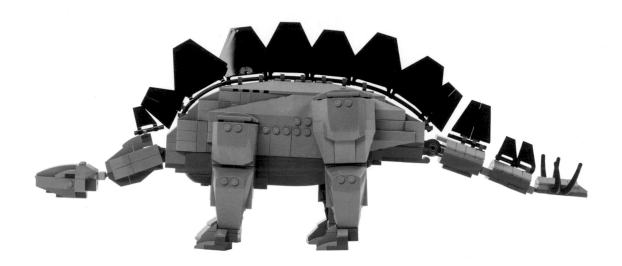

PIECES REQUIRED

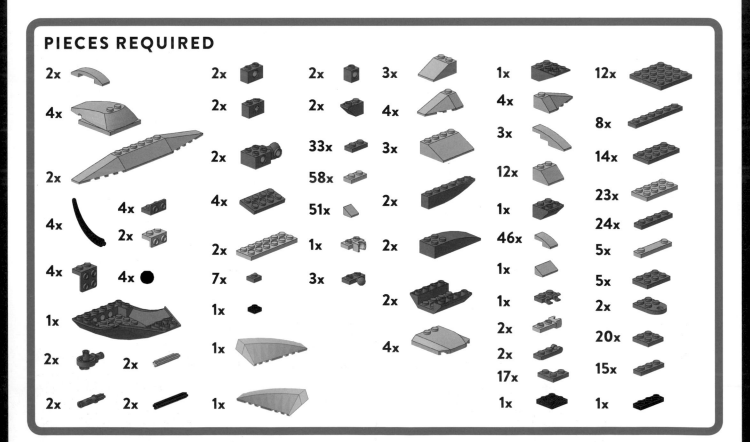

PIECES REQUIRED CONTINUED

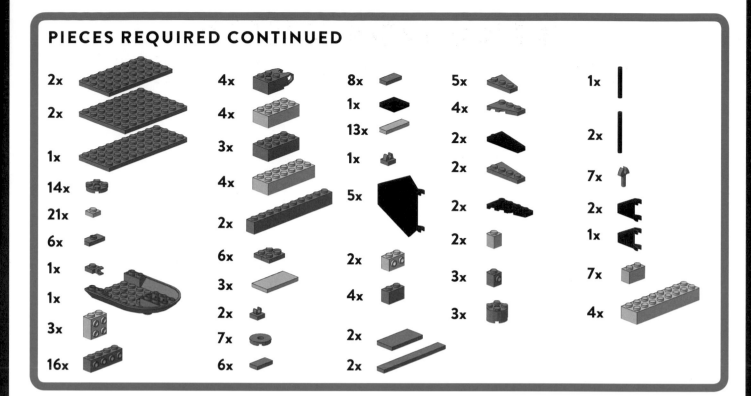

2x
2x
1x
14x
21x
6x
1x
1x
3x
16x

4x
4x
3x
4x
2x
6x
3x
2x
7x
6x

8x
1x
13x
1x
5x
2x
4x
2x
2x

5x
4x
2x
2x
2x
2x
2x
3x
3x

1x
2x
7x
2x
1x
7x
4x

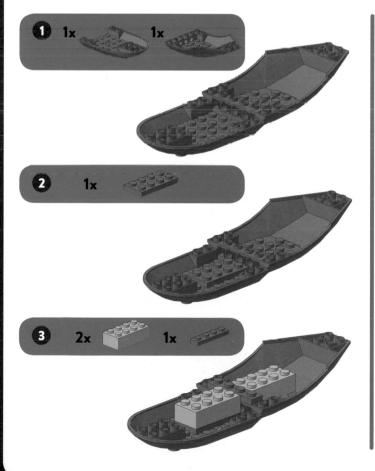

1 1x 1x

2 1x

3 2x 1x

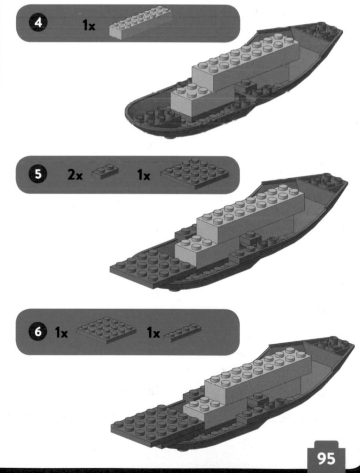

4 1x

5 2x 1x

6 1x 1x

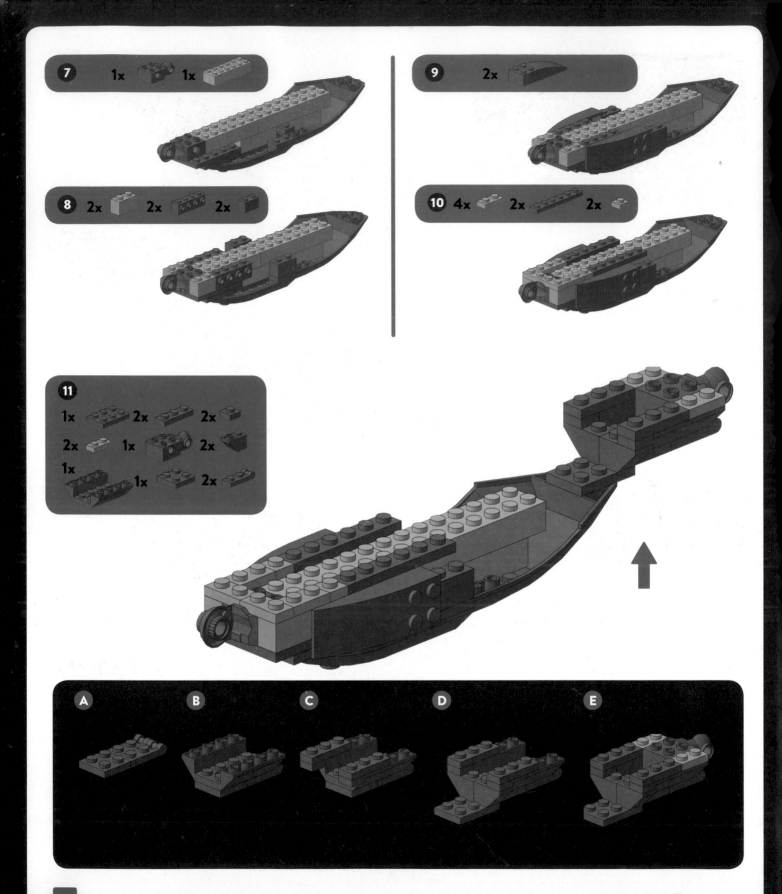

12
2x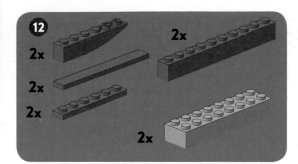
2x
2x
2x

13
5x

14
6x 2x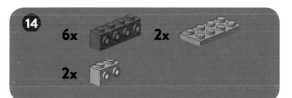
2x

15
1x 1x 1x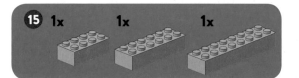

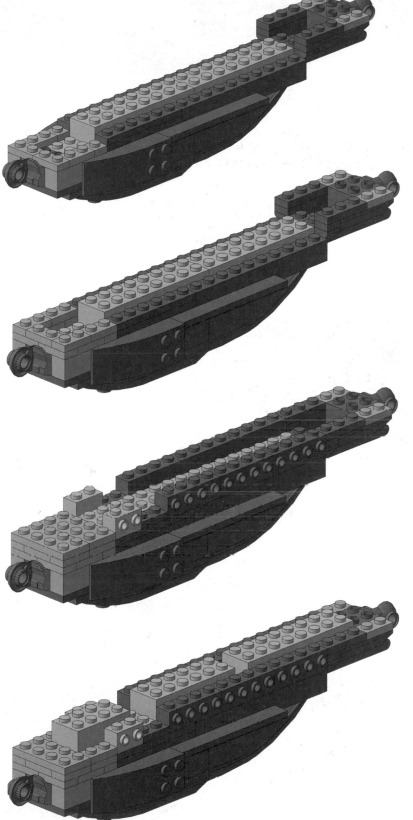

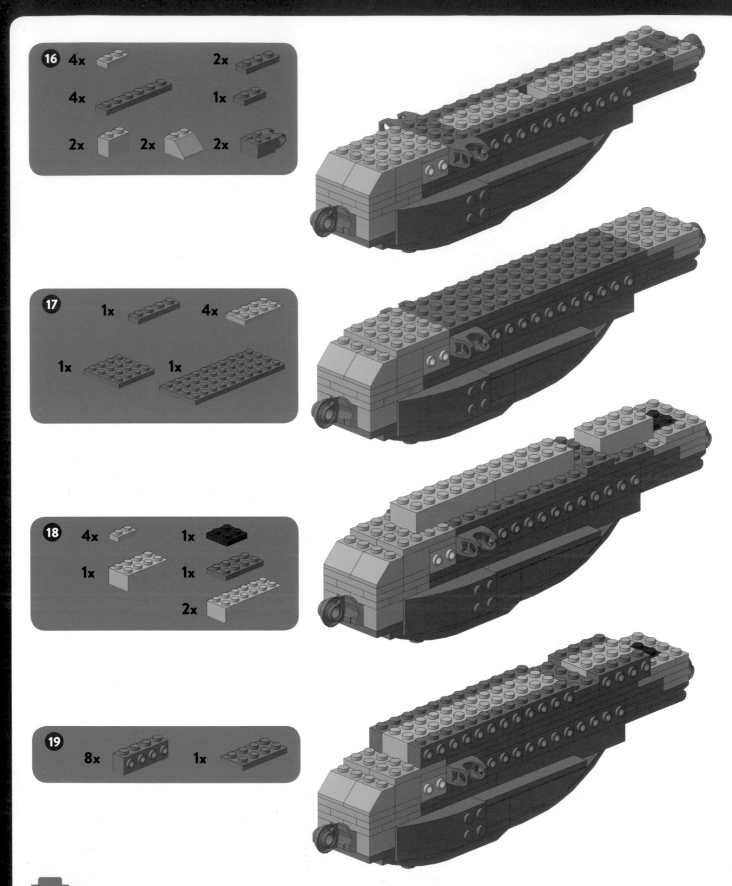

16
4x
2x
4x
1x
2x
2x
2x

17
1x
4x
1x
1x

18
4x
1x
1x
1x
2x

19
8x
1x

20

4x  4x 1x

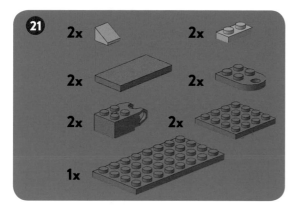

21
2x 2x
2x 2x
2x 2x
1x

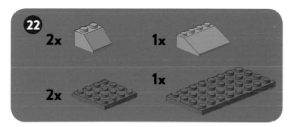

22
2x 1x
2x 1x

23
2x 2x

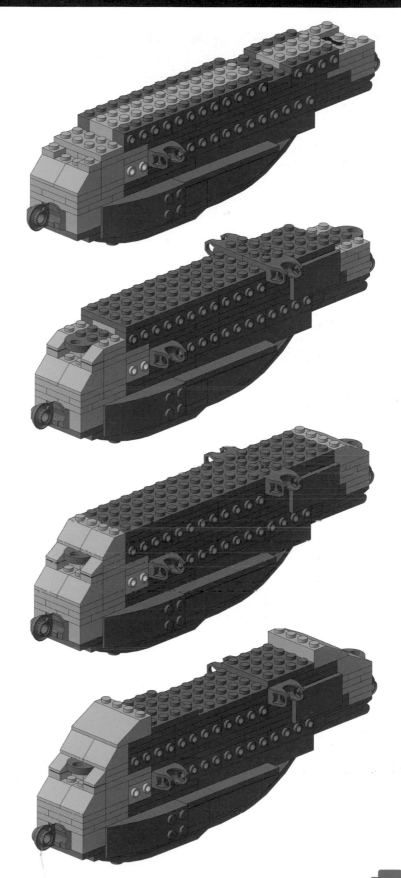

24 4x  2x 3x

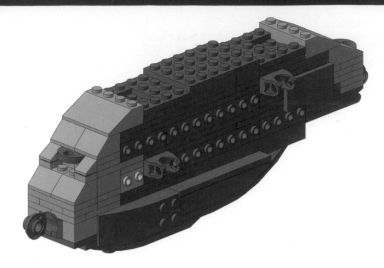

25 2x 6x

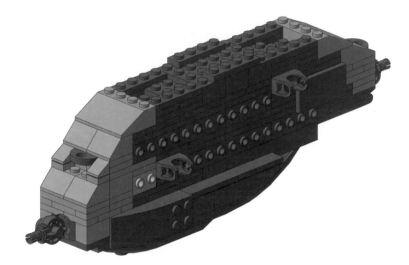

26 14x 7x 7x

A   B   C

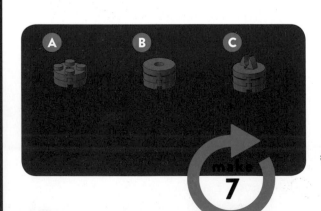

make
7

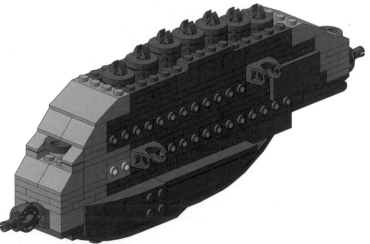

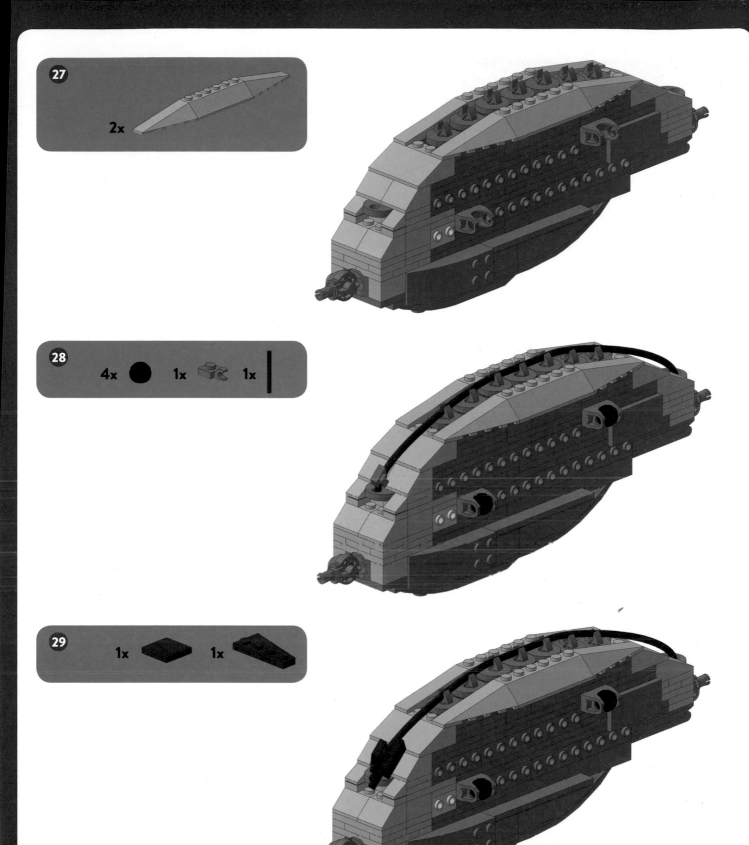

27 2x

28 4x ● 1x 🔧 1x |

29 1x ▬ 1x ▭

30

5x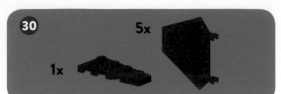

1x

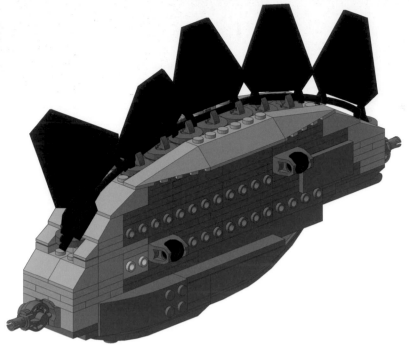

31

2x 2x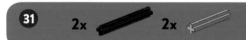

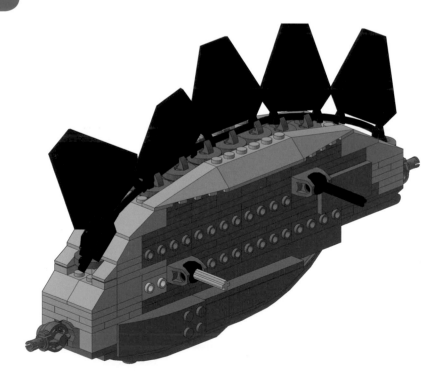

PART 1

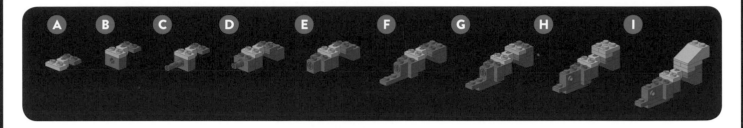

PART 2

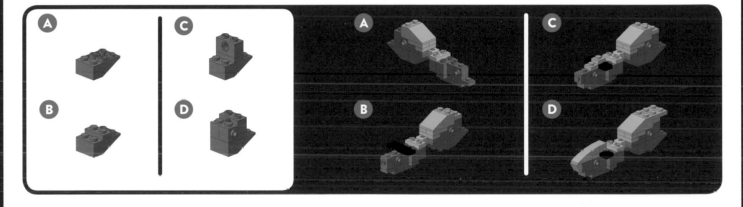

PART 3

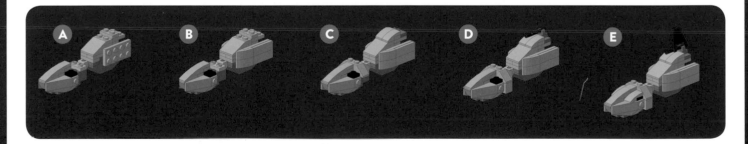

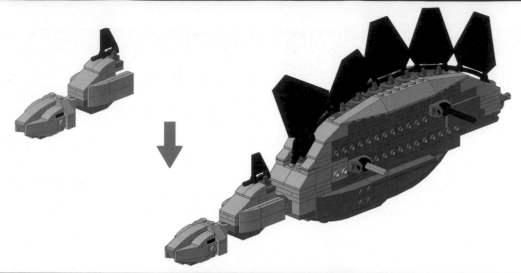

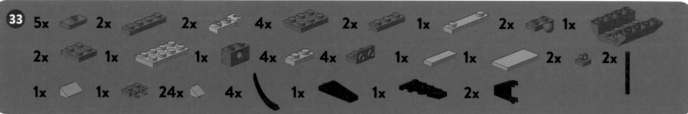

33 5x 2x 2x 4x 2x 1x 2x 1x

2x 1x 1x 4x 4x 1x 1x 1x 2x 2x

1x 1x 24x 4x 1x 1x 2x 1x

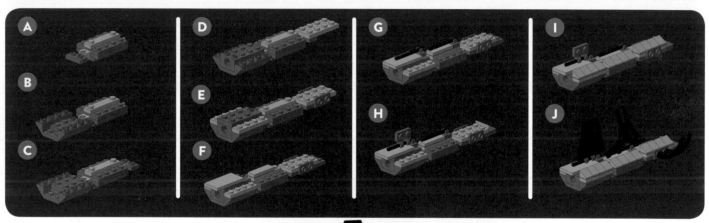

A
B
C
D
E
F
G
H
I
J

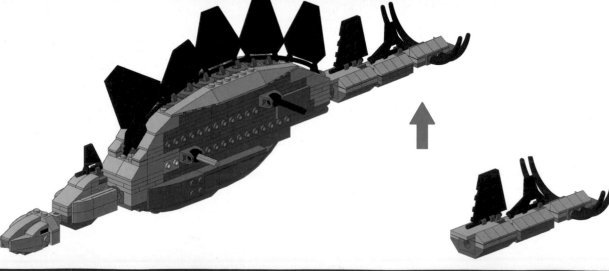

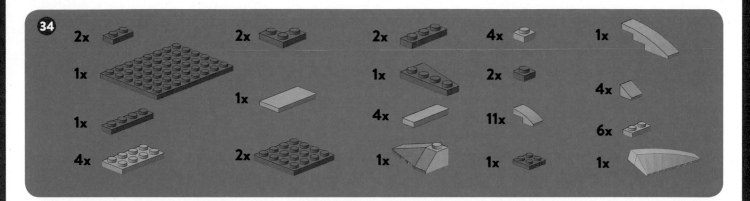

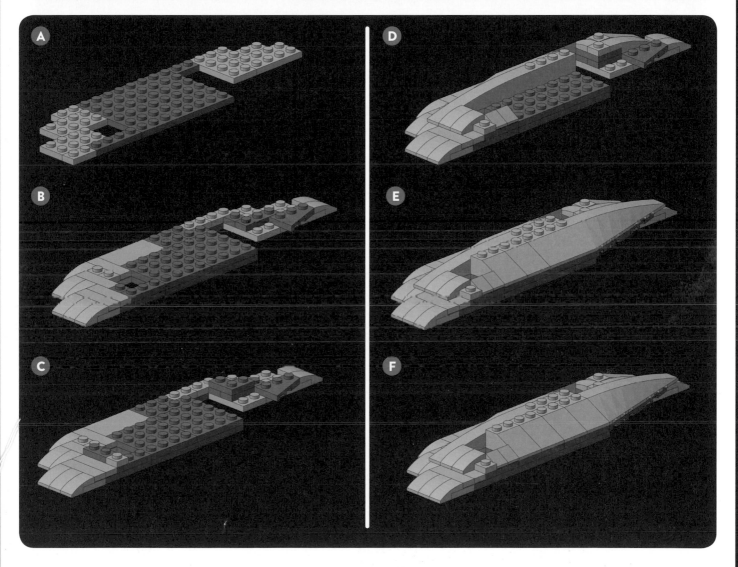

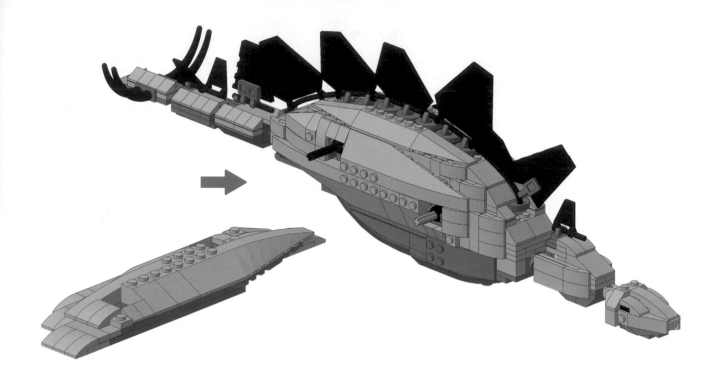

35 PART 1

A   B   C   D   E

PART 2

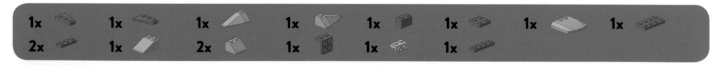

A   B   C   D   E

PART 3

PART 4

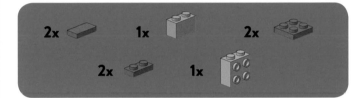

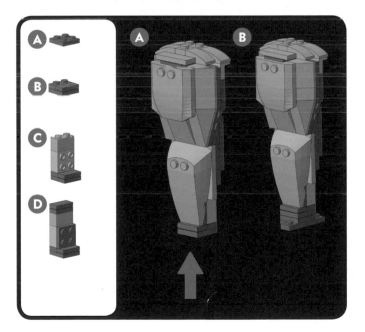

PART 5

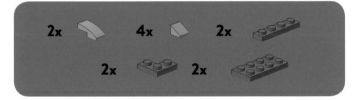

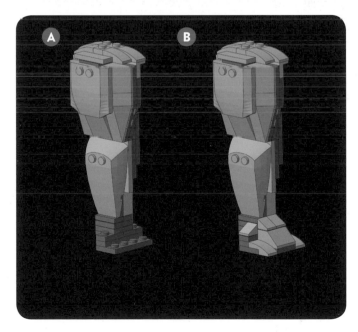

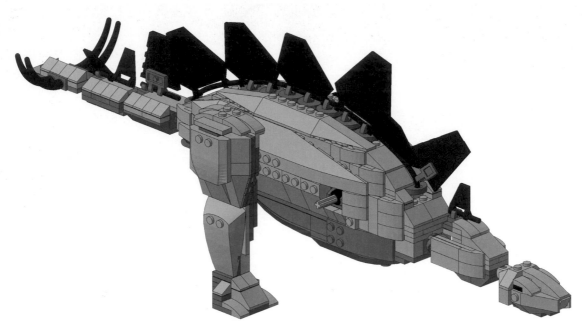

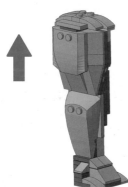

PART 1

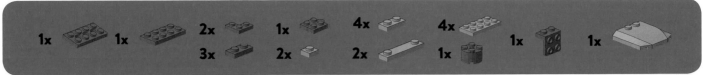

1x 1x 2x 3x 1x 2x 4x 2x 4x 1x 1x 1x

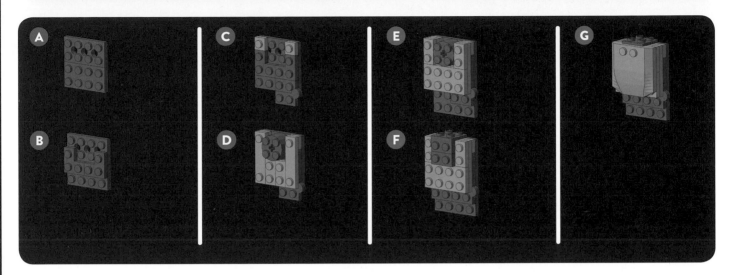

A

B

C

D

E

F

G

PART 2

1x 3x 1x 1x 1x 1x 1x 2x 2x

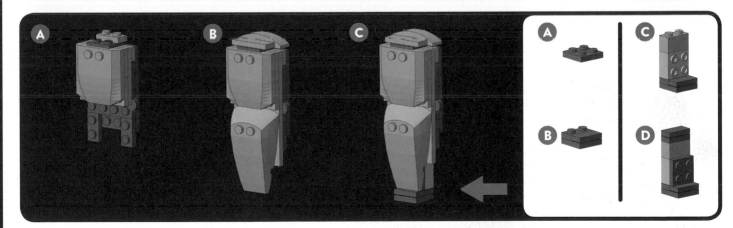

A B C

A B C D

PART 3

2x 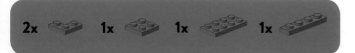 1x 1x 1x

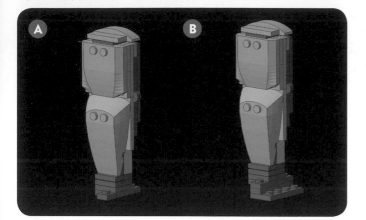

PART 4

1x  1x 4x 2x

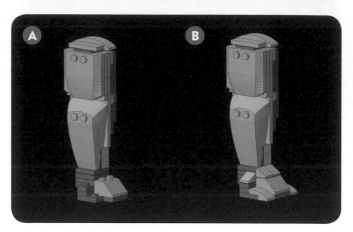

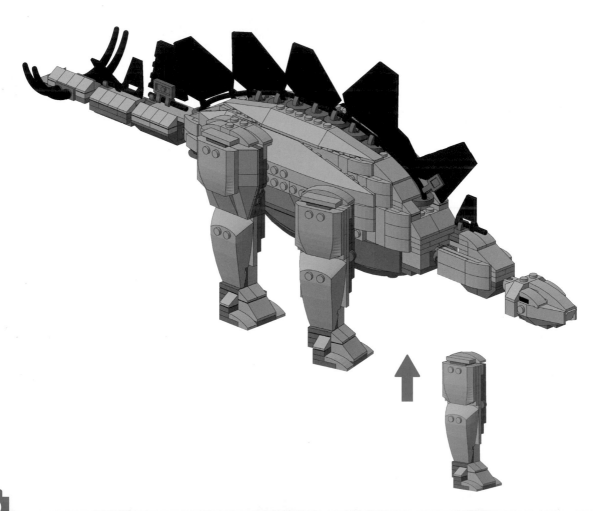

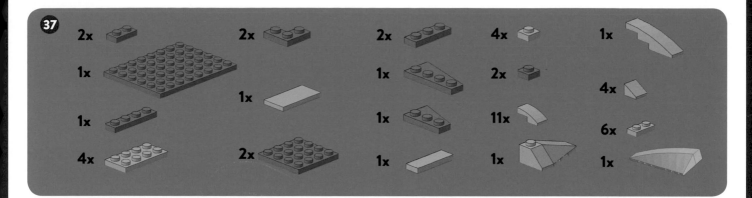

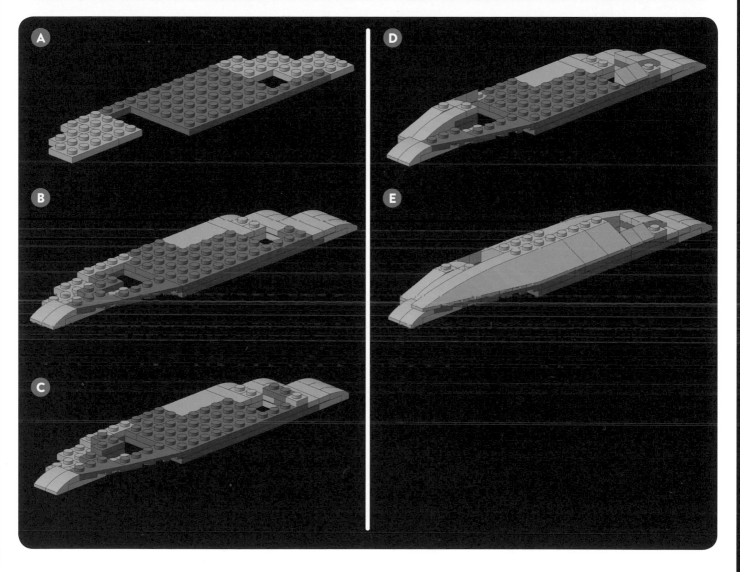

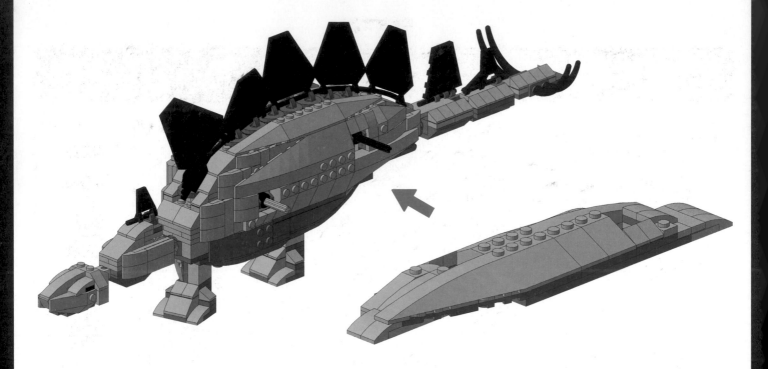

38

PART 1

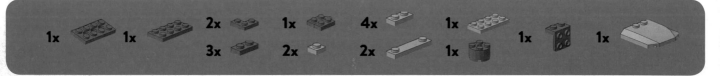

1x 1x 2x 1x 4x 1x 1x 1x
3x 2x 2x 1x

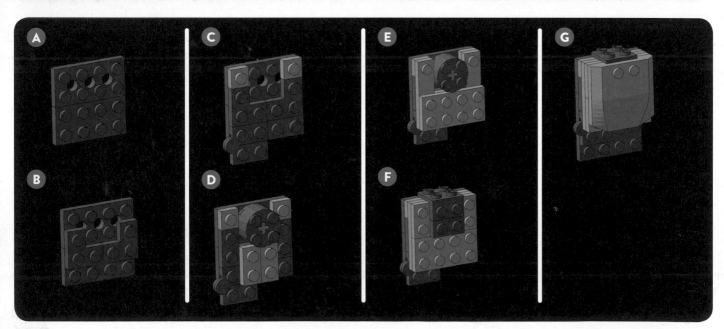

A B C D E F G

PART 2

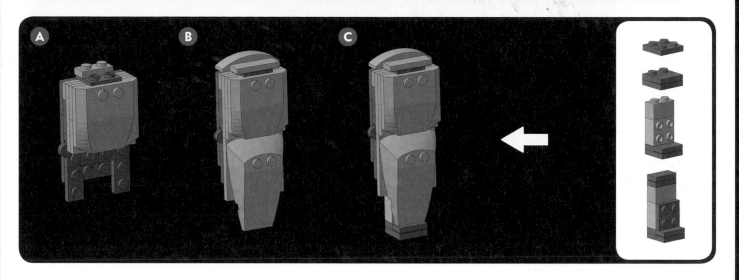

PART 3

PART 4

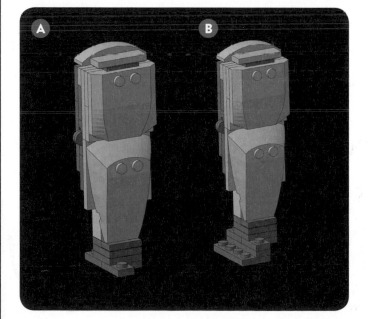

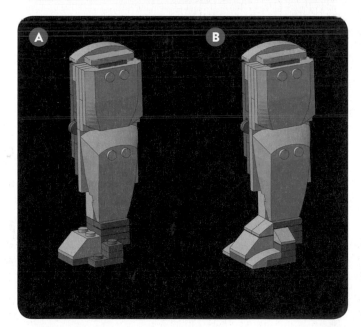

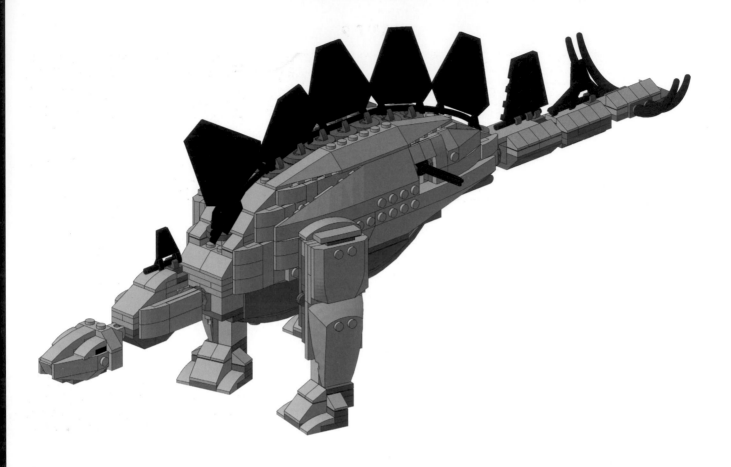

39

PART 1

1x	1x	1x	1x	1x
2x	2x	1x	1x	1x

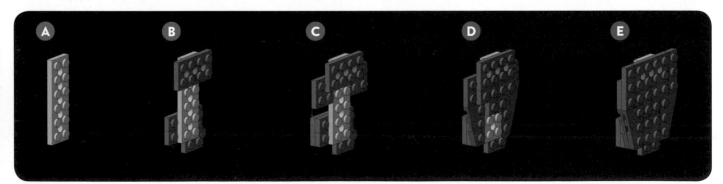

A   **B**   **C**   **D**   **E**

PART 2

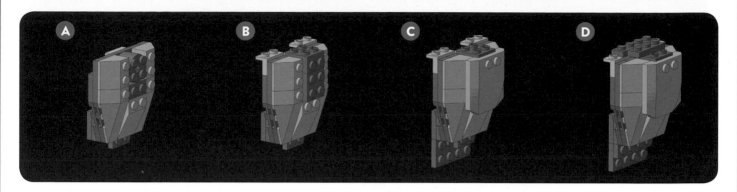

PART 3

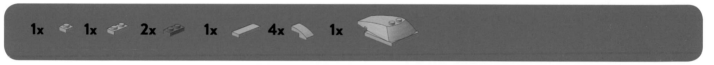

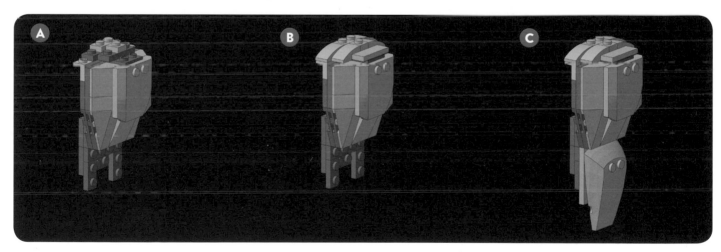

PART 4

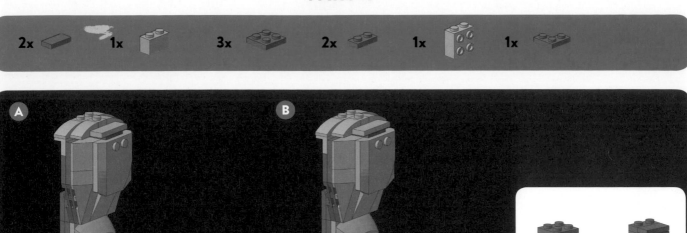

PART 5

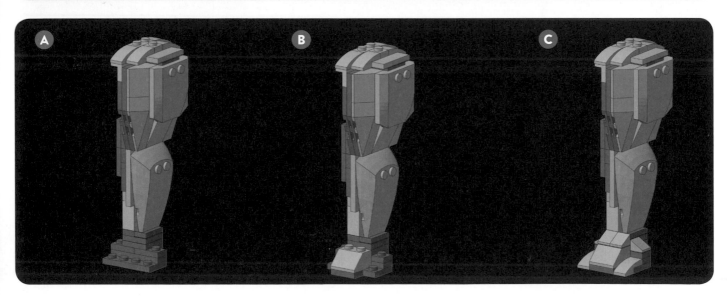

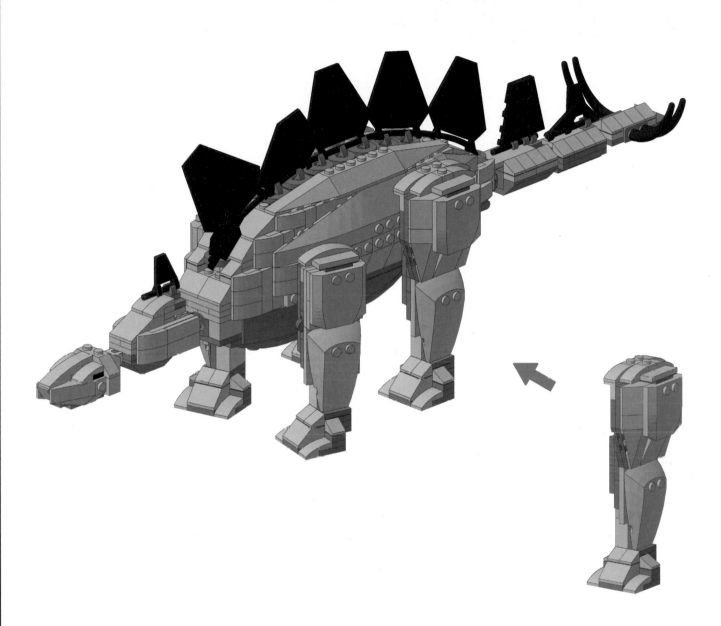

STEGOSAURUS

The spikes on Stegosaurus's tail were about 3 feet 3 inches (1 m) long. Paleontologists believe the dinosaur had a flexible tail and could have whipped the spikes at an attacker, causing serious damage. Around 1 in 10 Stegosaurus skeletons have damage to their tail spikes, which suggests they were often broken in combat.

CARNIVORES

Meat-eating, or carnivorous, dinosaurs were all members of the saurischian group. They were what paleontologists call theropods: dinosaurs that walked and ran on their hind legs and had short front limbs.

WHAT THEY LOOKED LIKE

Most theropods had sharp teeth and strong jaws, although the theropods that evolved to eat plants or insects had blunter teeth or none at all. Theropods had long, strong-muscled back legs. Like modern birds, most species had hollow bones, which made them lighter and a little more flexible. In fact, modern birds are descended from theropods. Theropods' short front limbs, or arms, had up to five fingers. Two or three fingers had large claws, while the fourth and fifth fingers, if they existed, were much smaller. They had five toes—three large and two small. The large, clawed toes pointed forward while the first smaller toe pointed backward. Although theropod means "beast-footed" in ancient Greek, theropod feet were rather like bird feet.

Many paleontologists think that all theropods had feathers on at least some parts of their skin. Some theropods, such as Archaeopteryx, were probably fully feathered. Others, which were less closely related to birds, probably had scalier skins more like a reptile's.

Perhaps the most famous of all dinosaur carnivores, the Tyranosaurus Rex hunted live prey over large distances and had a very powerful bite similar to that of an alligator.

DIFFERENT GROUPS

There were many different groups of theropods with different characteristics. Most theropods were tetanurans, which is ancient Greek for "stiff tails." Others, such as Ceratosaurus, had more flexible tails. Paleontologists believe they held their tails out behind them as they ran, balancing the weight of their body. The tetanurans are often divided into two main groups, although paleontologists often change their minds about them: the carnosaurs and the coelurosaurs. Carnosaurs (ancient Greek for "meat-eating lizards") were huge, fierce predators and among them were the largest carnivores ever to walk the Earth, including Allosaurus, which was around 32 feet (9.7 m) long, and Giganotosaurus, which may have reached 43 feet (13 m) long.

The coelurosaurs (ancient Greek for "hollow-tailed lizards") were generally smaller, although some did reach great sizes, and were more varied. Some of them were not meat-eaters. The coelurosaurs are more closely related to birds than the carnosaurs and were probably more feathery. Struthiomimus and the other ostrich-like dinosaurs were coelurosaurs. Tyrannosaurs had massive skulls and large teeth. Among the most well known is Tyrannosaurus Rex, because about fifty specimens, some quite complete and some just individual bones, have been found. Like some meat-eaters today, Tyannosaurus was probably both a predator and a scavenger, eating dead creatures that it found. The smallest carnivores were coelurosaurs, like four-winged Microraptor, which could be as little as 1.4 feet (42 cm) long—and most of that was the tail!

SPINOSAURUS

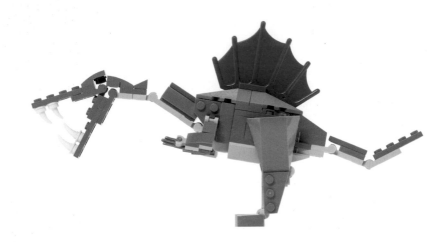

PIECES REQUIRED

2x	4x	2x	1x	4x
1x	2x	2x	2x	2x
2x	2x	1x	2x	2x
1x	1x	4x	6x	1x
2x	2x	3x	2x	
1x	2x	5x	1x	
4x	2x	2x	2x	
2x	3x	2x	1x	
	5x	2x	2x	
	1x	2x	4x	
	2x	1x		
	1x	2x		

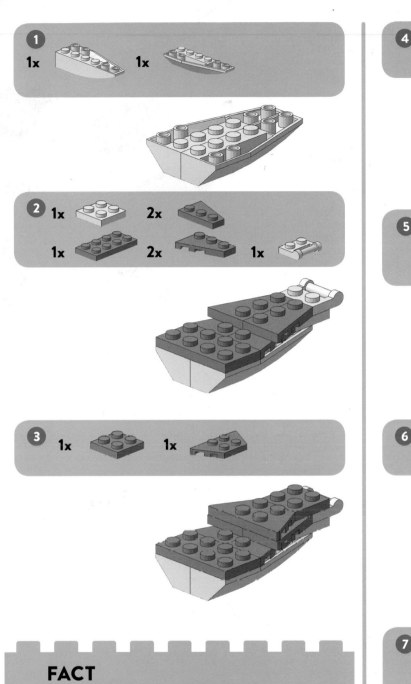

1
1x   1x

2
1x   2x
1x   2x   1x

3
1x   1x

FACT

- Spinosaurus was one of the largest carnivores ever to live, possibly larger than both Tyrannosaurus (around 40 ft/12.3 m long) and Giganotosaurus (around 43 ft/13 m long). It has been estimated that Spinosaurus was 41 to 59 feet (12.6 to 18 m) long and weighed 7.7 to 23 US tons (7 to 21 metric tons).

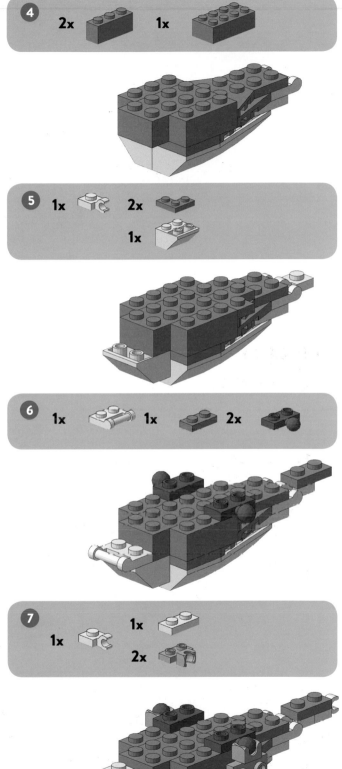

4
2x   1x

5
1x   2x
1x

6
1x   1x   2x

7
1x   1x
2x

123

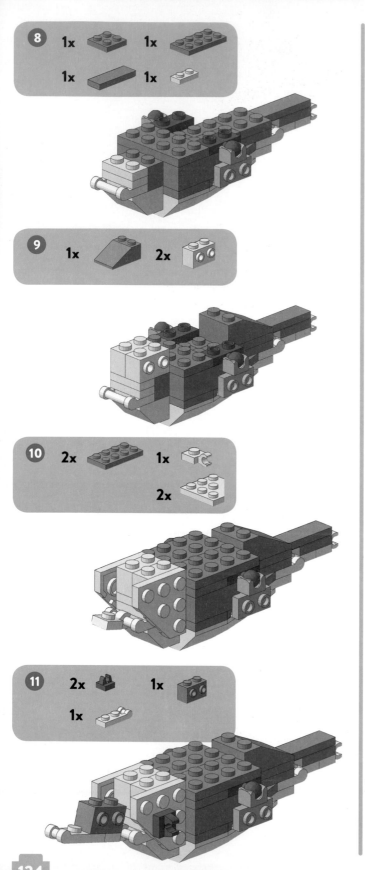

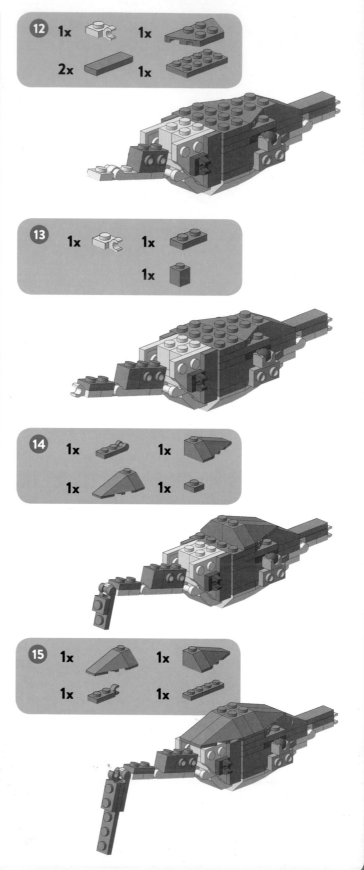

16

1x 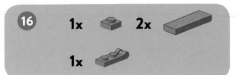 2x

1x

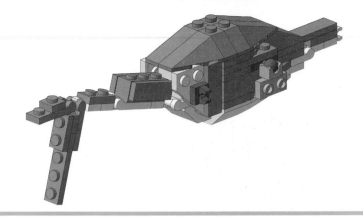

17

1x 1x

2x

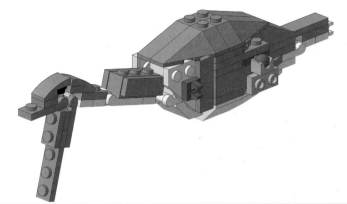

18

1x 1x

1x

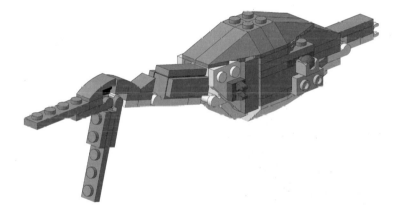

19

1x 4x

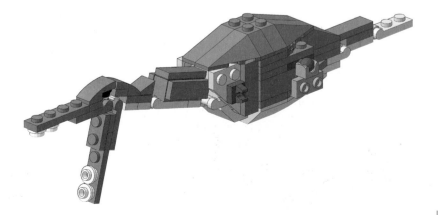

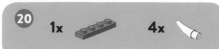

20   1x 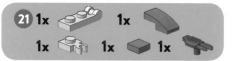   4x

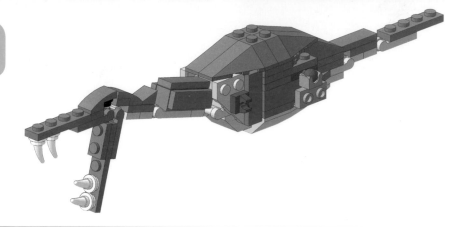

21 1x   1x
    1x   1x   1x

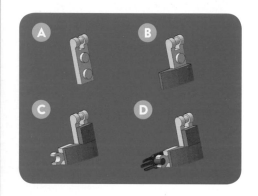

A   B

C   D

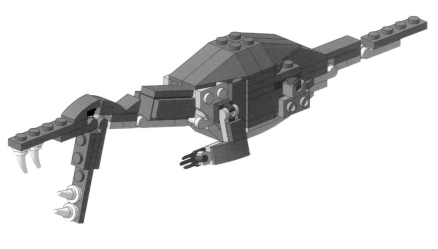

22 1x   1x
    1x   1x   1x

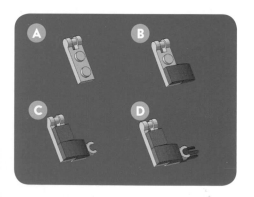

A   B

C   D

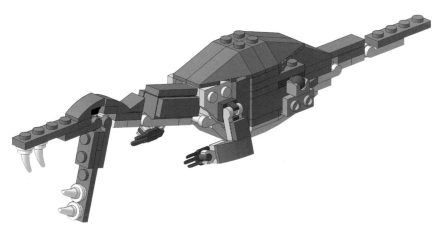

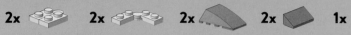

PART 1

PART 2

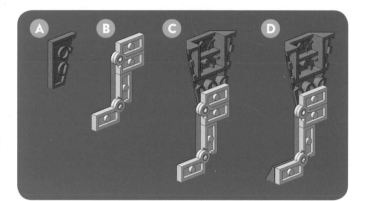

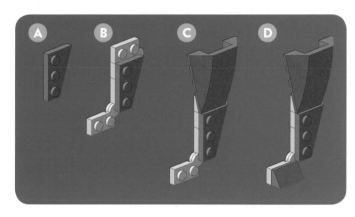

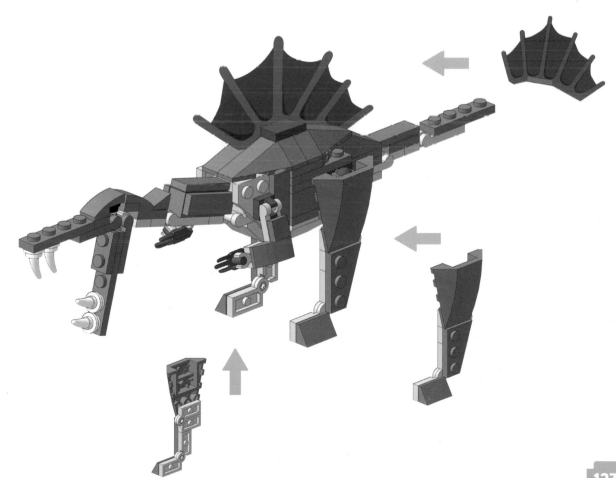

SPINOSAURUS

Bony spines down Spinosaurus's back grew to 64 inches (1.65 m) long. The spines were probably covered in skin, forming a sail-like structure, or they may have been covered in fat to form a hump, like a camel's. Paleontologists are not sure what the sail or hump was for, but it may have been for attracting a mate during courtship.

HERBIVORES

More dinosaurs were plant-eaters, called herbivores, than carnivores. Herbivores were also more varied than carnivores. They belonged to both the saurischian and ornithischian groups. Some walked on four legs while others walked on their hind legs.

DIFFERENT FEATURES

If all the dinosaurs in a habitat had been trying to eat the same type of plant, the food supply would have run out quickly. Some herbivores were probably grazers, like today's sheep and cows, cropping low-growing vegetation from the ground. Others were browsers, breaking off higher-growing leaves and twigs, like today's giraffes. Being taller or shorter, or having a longer neck than other herbivores, would have helped different species specialize in eating different plants. This is one of the reasons why some herbivores, such as Diplodocus, were

Herbivores were usually slower movers, as they did not have to chase their prey.

immense, while others, such as Albertadromeus, were only about 5 feet (1.6 m) long.

Herbivores did not need long, sharp teeth or claws to attack prey. However, some herbivores, such as Therizinosaurus, did have long claws. Therizinosaurus's 3.3-foot (1 m) claws were probably used for grabbing and slicing plants, as well as defense. Iguanodon had large thumb spikes, which may have been used to break into fruits and seeds.

The plants that the dinosaurs ate were much less nutritious than the flowering plants of today. This meant that the dinosaurs had to eat all the time and that food stayed in their stomachs for a long time so their bodies could absorb all the nutrients.

The different-shaped teeth and jaws of different species tell paleontologists about what sorts of plants they ate: some possibly ate only soft water plants, while others could grind down twigs. The huge sauropods, which were saurischians, could not chew, as they did not have cheeks to hold food nor grinding back teeth. Instead, they had peg-like teeth that raked leaves from trees. The tough plant material was then broken down in their gigantic stomachs. They would swallow stones, just like modern plant-eating birds swallow grit, to help grind up the food. Most ornithischians had leaf-shaped teeth in their cheeks for grinding leaves and stems. Many had a toothless, horned beak at the front of the jaw for breaking off plants. The dinosaurs with the most teeth were the duckbills, or hadrosaurs, which had many hundreds of teeth growing through the jaw to replace those that were constantly being worn down—up to 960 of them!

HERDING

Scientists think that herbivores, and possibly all dinosaurs, lived in herds. Some of their body features (as well as many trackways that have been found) tell us about behavior within their herds. It is thought that the horns on the heads of Triceratops had more to do with relationships within the herd than defense against predators. Like male reindeer and rhinoceros beetles today, male Triceratops may have had fierce battles with each other. The winner would have had a more powerful position in the herd, and more opportunities to mate with females. Dinosaurs with very elaborate neck frills, such as Centrosaurus, may have used them for display, to warn off other males, or to attract females.

Pachycephalosaurs (from the ancient Greek for "thick-headed lizards") had a particularly hard, dome-shaped skull. These may have been useful in head-butting contests between males.

BRACHIOSAURUS

PIECES REQUIRED

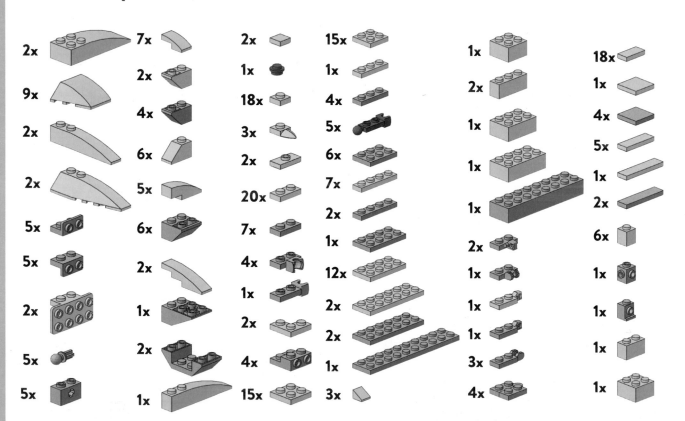

2x	7x	2x	15x	1x	18x
9x	2x	1x	1x	2x	1x
2x	4x	18x	4x	1x	4x
2x	6x	3x	5x	1x	5x
5x	5x	2x	6x	1x	1x
5x	6x	20x	7x	1x	2x
2x	2x	7x	2x	2x	6x
5x	1x	4x	1x	1x	1x
2x	2x	1x	12x	1x	1x
5x		2x	2x	1x	1x
5x	1x	4x	2x	3x	
		15x	1x	4x	1x
			3x		

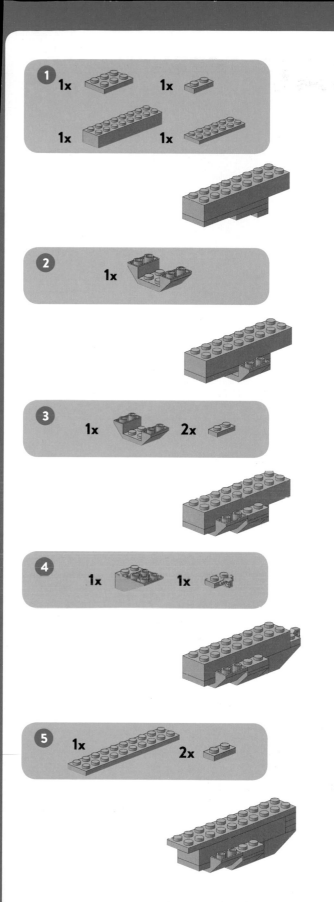

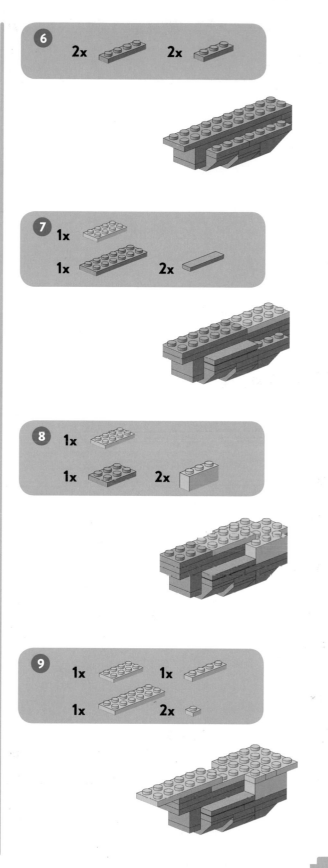

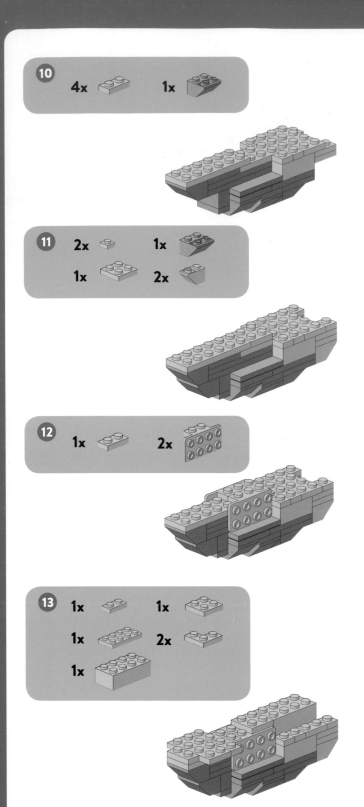

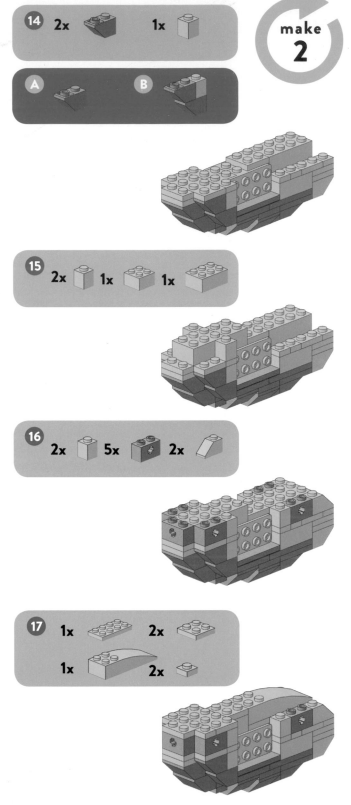

10 4x 1x

11 2x 1x 1x 2x

12 1x 2x

13 1x 1x 1x 1x 2x 1x

14 2x 1x

A **B**

15 2x 1x 1x

16 2x 5x 2x

17 1x 2x 1x 2x

18

2x 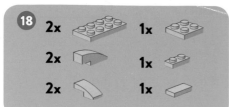 1x

2x 1x

2x 1x

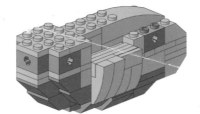

A | C
B | D

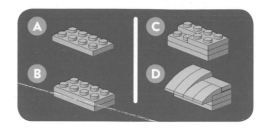

19

2x 1x

2x 1x

2x 1x

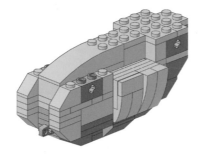

A | C
B | D

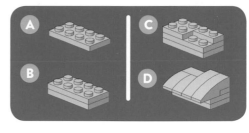

20

1x 2x

1x

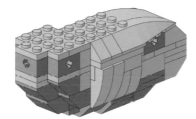

A B

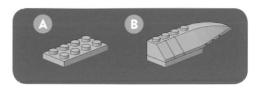

21

1x 2x

1x 1x

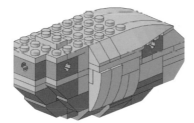

A B

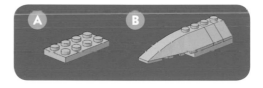

22

1x 1x

1x 1x

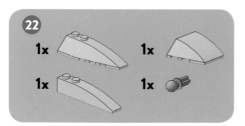

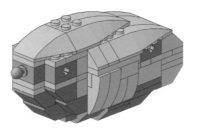

23

2x 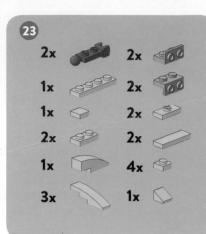 2x
1x 2x
1x 2x
2x 2x
1x 4x
3x 1x

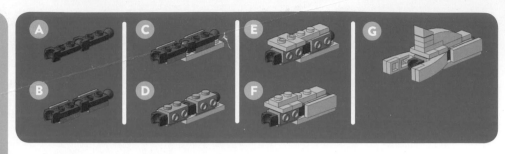

A B C D E F G

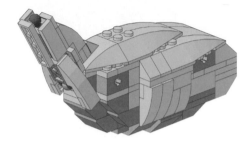

24

1x 1x

A B

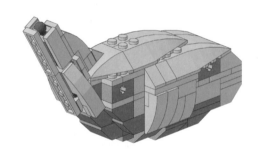

25

1x 1x
1x 1x
3x

A B C D E

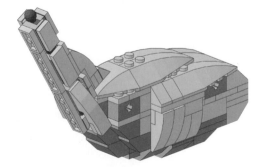

1x 1x
1x 1x
1x 2x

A   B   C   D   E

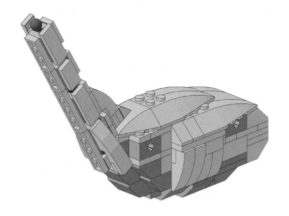

1x 1x
1x 1x
2x 1x

A   B   C   D   E

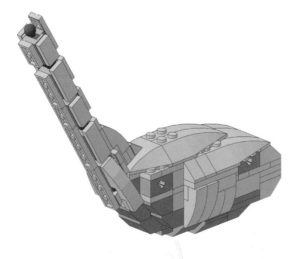

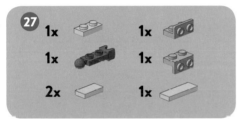

FACT

- Brachiosaurus may have been about 85 feet (26 m) long and could have stood 41 feet (12.6 m) tall with its neck extended. It may have weighed as much as 61 US tons (56 metric tons)—the same as 10 African elephants. For a long time, Brachiosaurus was believed to be the heaviest dinosaur, but sauropods such as Argentinosaurus probably weighed a little more.

28

1x  2x
2x 1x 1x

A B C D

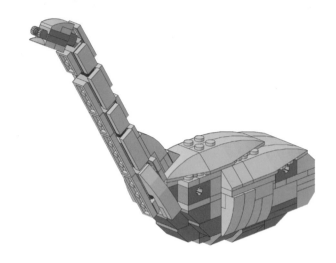

29

1x 1x
2x 1x
1x 2x
1x 2x
1x

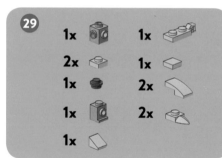

A B C D E F

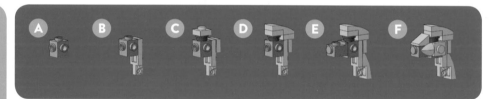

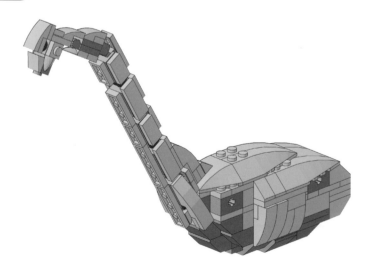

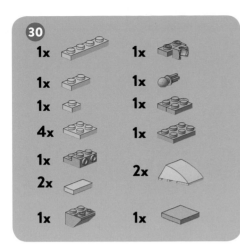

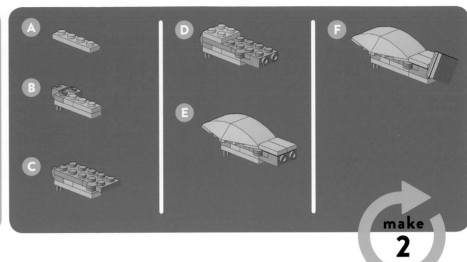

make
2

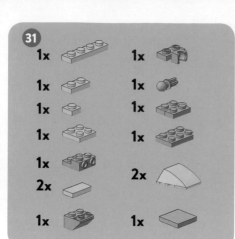

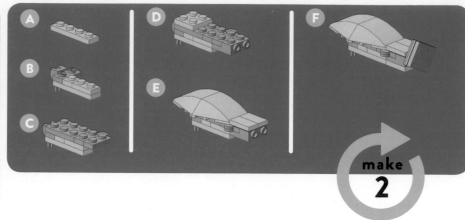

make
2

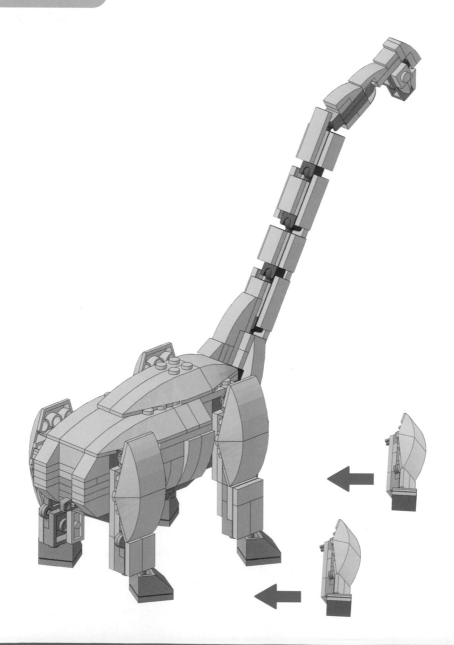

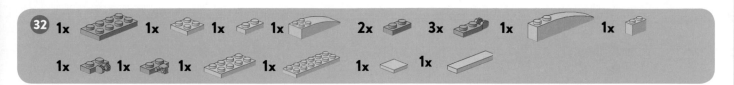

PART 1

PART 2

PART 3

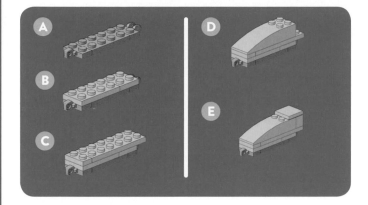

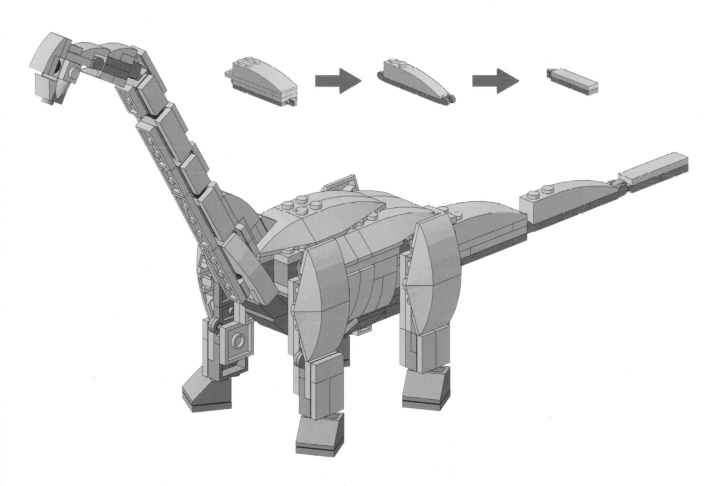

BRACHIOSAURUS

An adult Brachiosaurus probably had to eat as much as 880 pounds (400 kg) of plants every day. It is likely to have fed on coniferous (needle-leafed) trees and stiff-leafed gingkoes and cycads. It had a wide mouth and thick jawbones with spoon-shaped teeth, which would have been suited to stripping these tough plants.

DIPLODOCUS

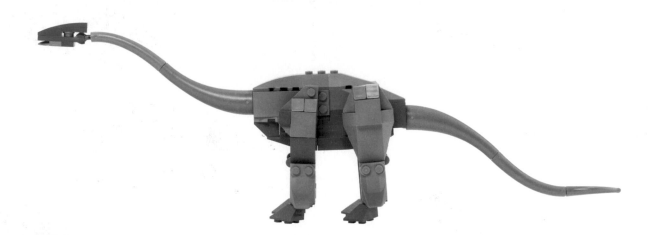

PIECES REQUIRED

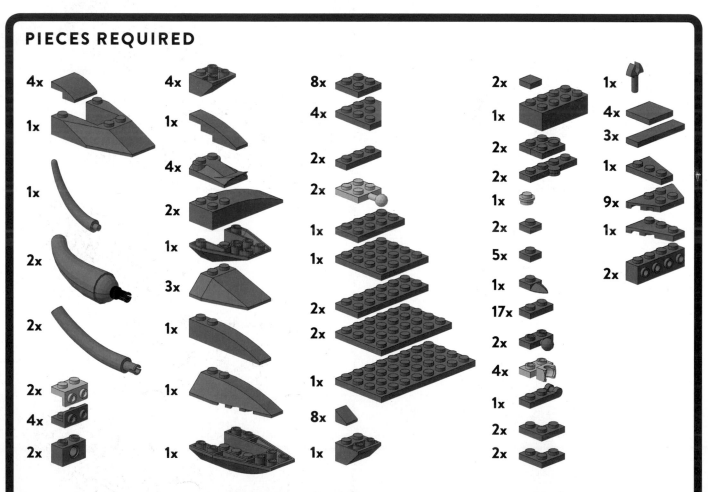

4x

1x

1x

2x

2x

2x

4x

2x

4x

1x

4x

2x

1x

3x

1x

1x

8x

4x

2x

2x

1x

1x

2x

2x

1x

8x

1x

2x

1x

2x

2x

1x

2x

5x

1x

17x

2x

4x

1x

2x

2x

1x

4x

3x

1x

9x

1x

2x

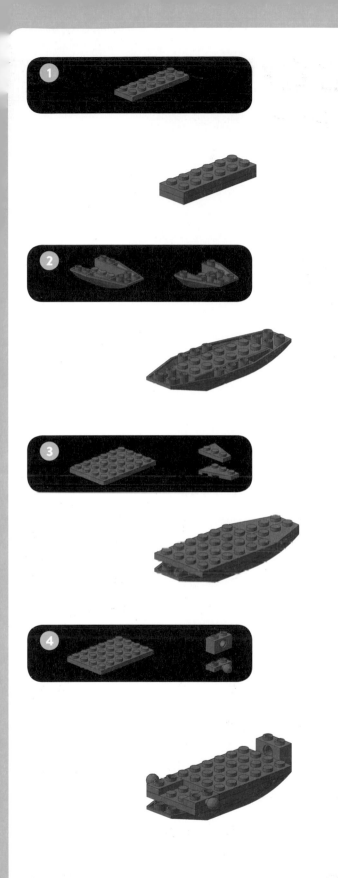

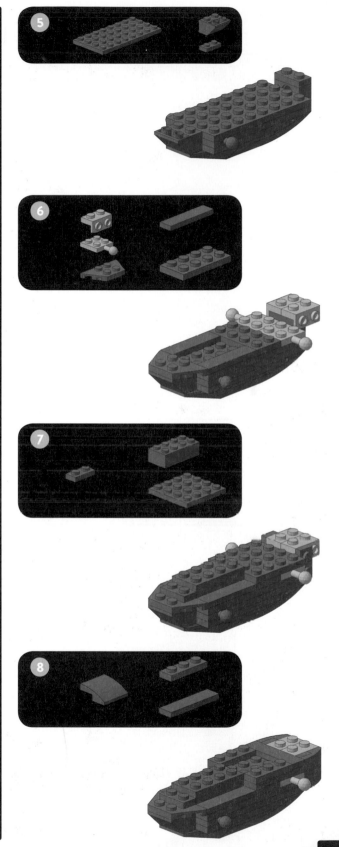

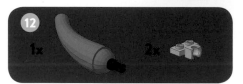

FACT

- Diplodocus's extra-long tail contained about 80 bones. The tail probably helped to balance the dinosaur's weight as it walked. It may also have been used for defense, as it could have been cracked like a whip.

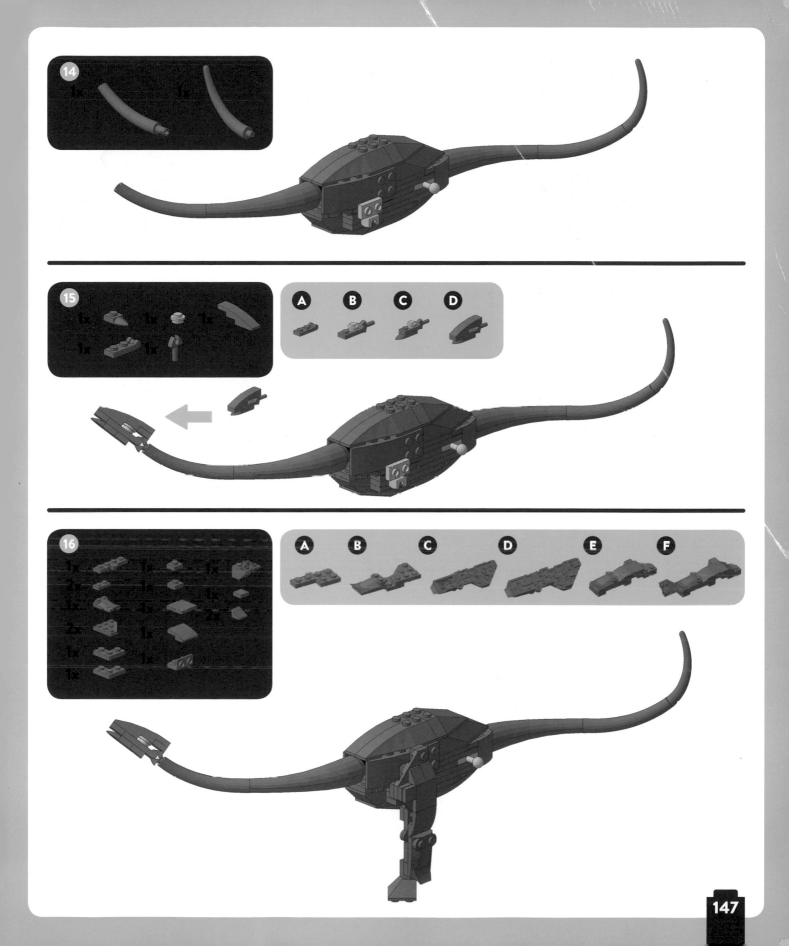

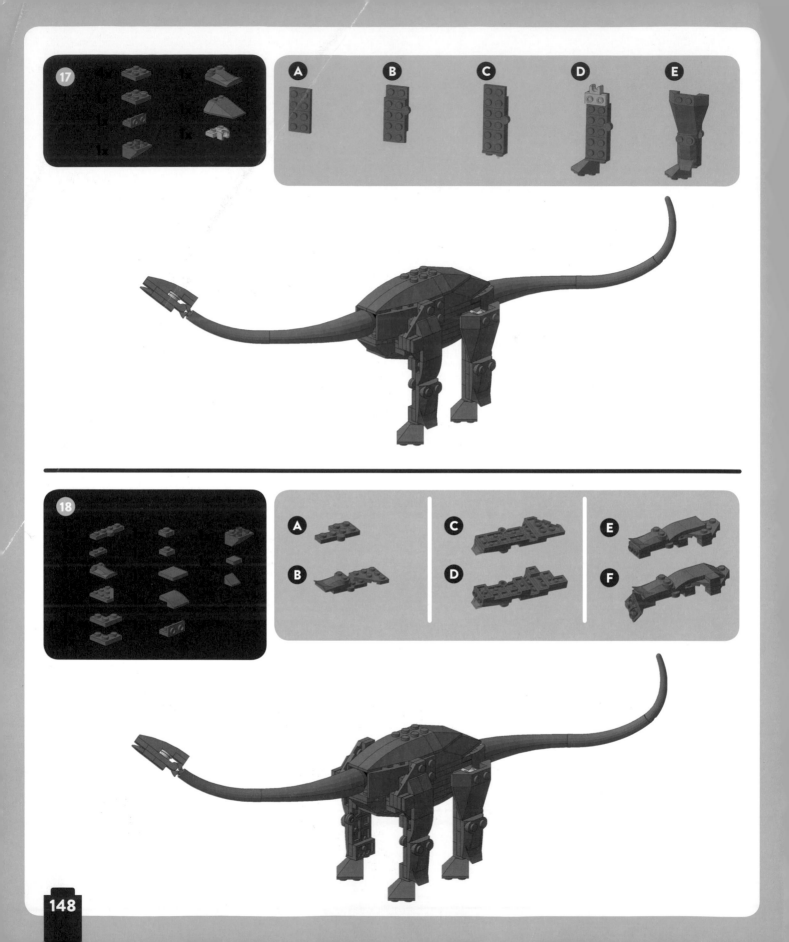

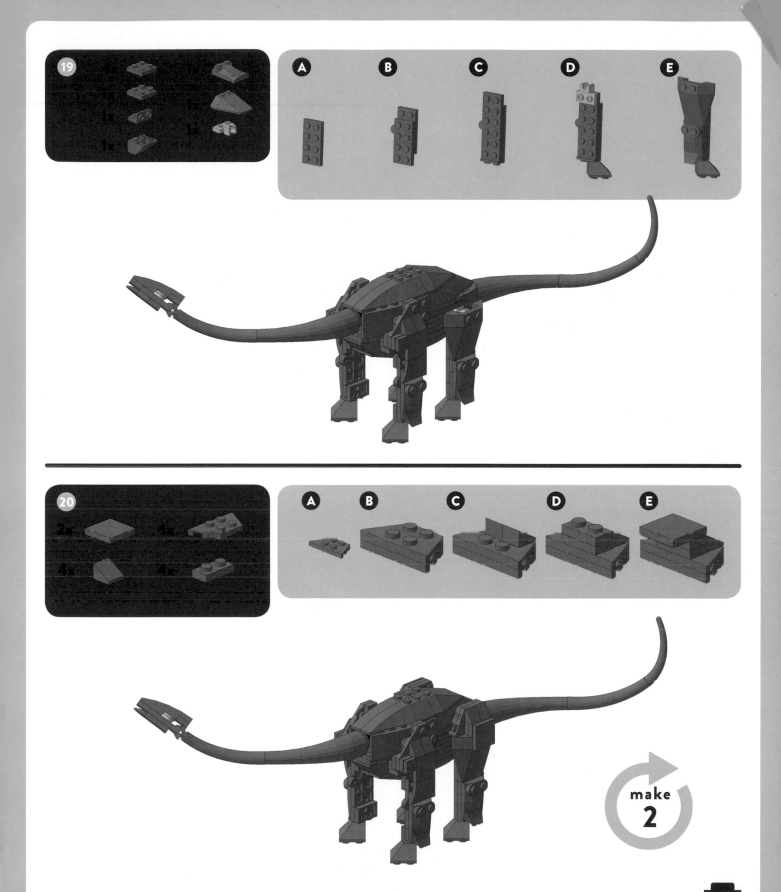

make
2

DIPLODOCUS

Diplodocus was one of the longest dinosaurs known at up to 105 feet (32 m) long in total. Its neck made up about 26 feet (8 m) of this length, while its tail was a full 45 feet (14 m) long. Diplodocus may have weighed around 18 US tons (16 metric tons), far less than the shorter Brachiosaurus, as it was much more slender.

NON-DINOSAURS

At the same time as dinosaurs walked the Earth, other extraordinary reptiles swam in the seas, soared in the air, and scuttled on land. Some prehistoric reptiles preyed on fish, birds, insects, amphibians, or mammals, while others were plant-eaters.

IN THE AIR

Insects were the first animals to fly around 350 million years ago. The most important flying animals at the time of the dinosaurs were the pterosaurs. Pterosaur bones were hollow, making them more lightweight and suited to flight. Pterosaur wings were made of skin, muscle, and other strong tissues. They stretched from the long fourth finger on each arm, along the sides of the body, joining to the ankle. The smallest pterosaurs had wingspans (from wingtip to wingtip) of just 10 inches (25 cm). The largest pterosaurs, such as Quetzalcoatlus, had wingspans of at least 36 feet (11 m). With wings this size, Quetzalcoatlus might have flown at 80 miles (128 km) per hour, covering distances of thousands of miles. Early pterosaurs had sharp teeth, but some later species evolved to have toothless beaks.

The Elasmosaurus was a plesiosaur with an extremely long neck from the Late Cretaceous Period. Originally, paleontologists placed the head on the wrong end of the skeleton, assuming that the neck could not be that long!

IN THE SEAS

Reptiles evolved on land. It was not until the Triassic Period, around 250 million years ago, that the first reptiles adapted to life in water. As reptiles need to breathe air, marine (sea-living) reptiles have to surface from time to time. Among the earliest marine reptiles were the placodonts and nothosaurs. These were not very different-looking from land-living reptiles, with sprawling legs and heavy bodies. However, they had webbed feet to help them paddle through water. These creatures probably moved between shallow waters and the shore. The first marine reptiles to live their whole lives in water, surfacing only to breathe, were the ichthyosaurs. They had bodies with a similar shape to modern dolphins, and they gave birth to live young rather than laying eggs like other reptiles. The ichthyosaurs were extinct by about 90 million years ago.

Another group of marine reptiles was the plesiosaurs, which evolved about 205 million years ago. They had long, flexible necks, paddle-like flippers, and streamlined bodies. They ate fish and squid. Sea lizards, turtles, and crocodile-like reptiles also lived at the same time as the dinosaurs. Mosasaurs were among the largest of the sea lizards, with Mosasaurus reaching lengths of 56 feet (17 m). Unlike the dinosaurs, plesiosaurs, and mosasaurs, the turtles and crocodile-like reptiles survived the mass extinction at the end of the Cretaceous Period.

SARCOSUCHUS

PIECES REQUIRED

6x		1x		2x		2x
8x		2x		4x		1x
2x		32x		38x		2x
4x		2x		2x		32x
1x		12x		16x		1x
3x		6x		3x		1x
1x		1x		8x		2x
1x		4x		12x		2x
1x		2x		8x		1x
1x		1x		2x		1x
1x		1x		1x		3x
7x		1x		4x		3x
1x		1x		1x		1x
9x		8x		3x		

1
1x 1x
1x 1x

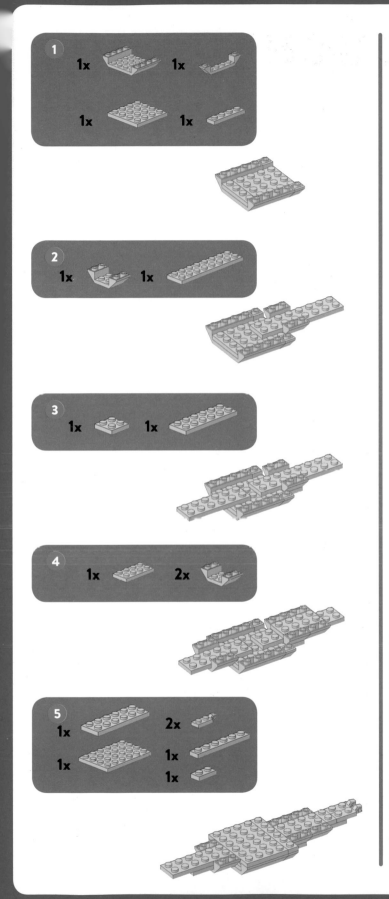

2
1x 1x

3
1x 1x

4
1x 2x

5
1x 2x
1x 1x
      1x

6
1x 1x 1x
    1x
1x 2x 1x

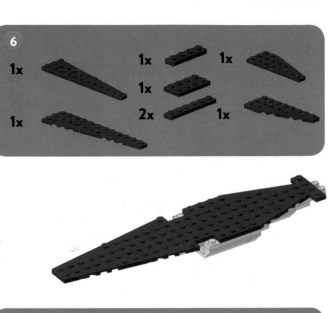

7
1x 2x 2x
1x 1x 2x

FACT

- Living in tropical lakes and rivers, Sarcosuchus may have had a diet like today's Nile crocodile, including fish, insects, shellfish, amphibians, and small reptiles. Some paleontologists think that Sarcosuchus would have left the water to hunt dinosaurs, but others think that its relatively slim jaws and small teeth would have meant that it stuck to more manageable-sized prey.

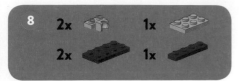

8   2x   1x   2x   1x

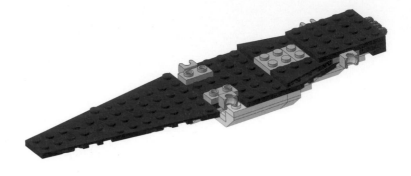

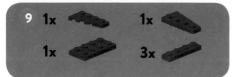

9   1x   1x   1x   3x

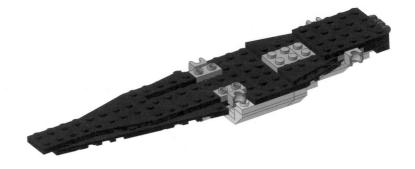

10   6x   14x

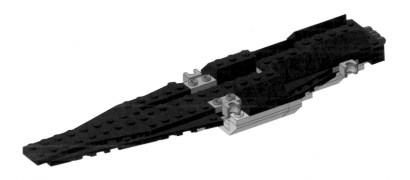

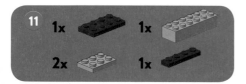

11   1x   1x   2x   1x

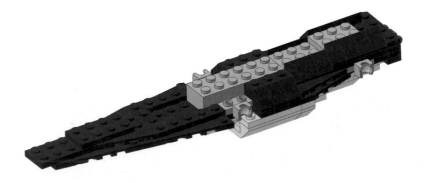

12
1x 2x
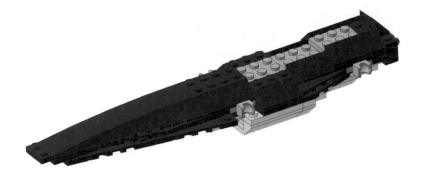

13
2x
4x 1x
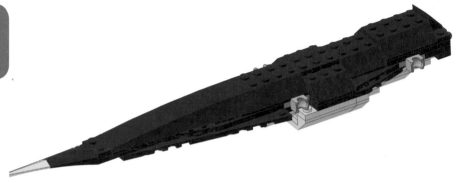

14
38x
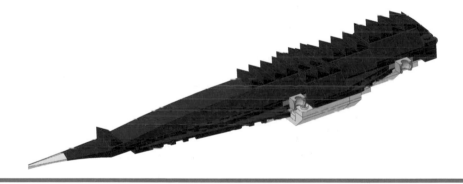

15
1x 2x
2x 2x

A B C

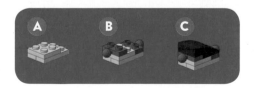

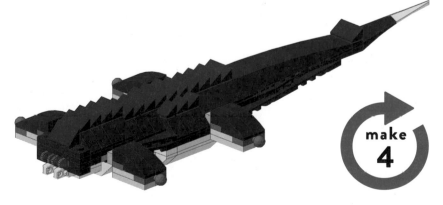

make
4

1x 3x 1x 1x
3x 1x

A B C

make
4

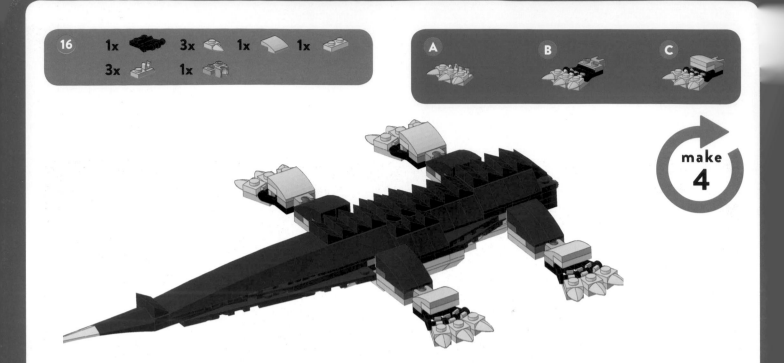

1x 1x 1x 2x 1x 1x 1x 16x 16x

A B C D

make
16

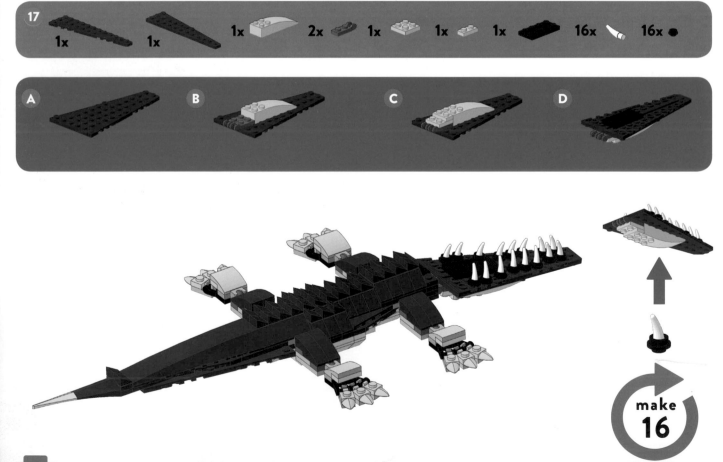

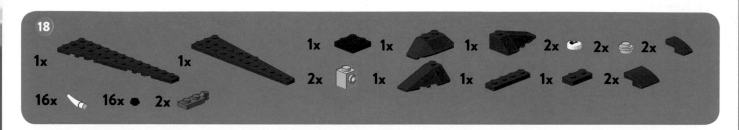

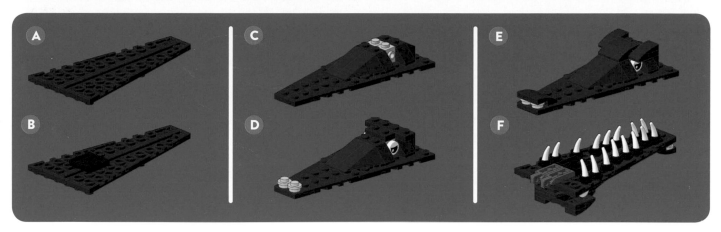

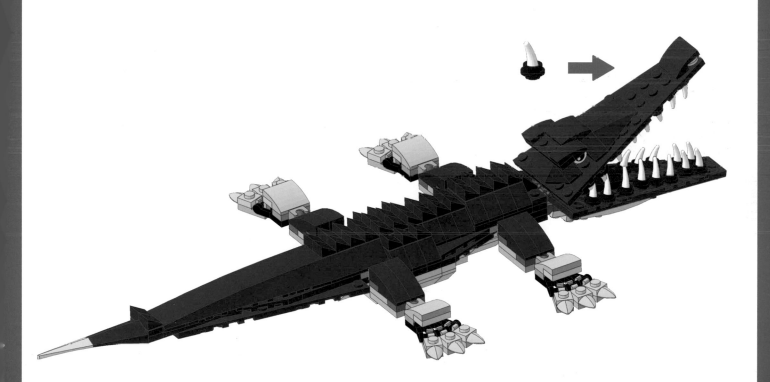

SARCOSUCHUS

Sarcosuchus's name means "flesh crocodile." It was one of the largest crocodile-like reptiles ever to live, weighing as much as 8.8 US tons (8 metric tons) and reaching 38 feet (11.7 m) long, which is more than twice as long as the saltwater crocodile, the largest reptile alive today.

ARCHAEOPTERYX

PIECES REQUIRED

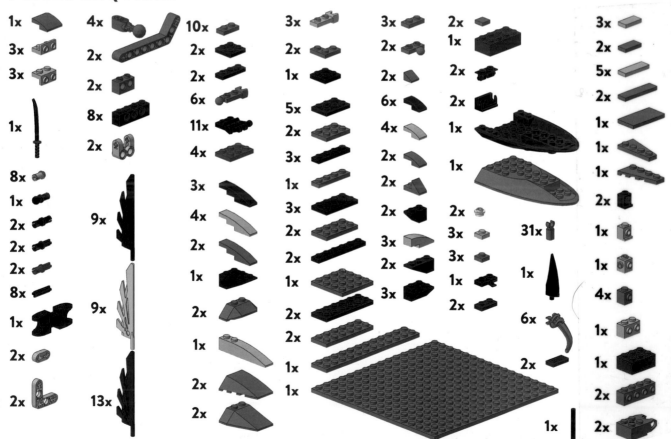

1x   4x   10x   3x   3x   2x   3x
3x   2x   2x   2x   2x   1x   2x
3x   2x   2x   1x   2x   2x   5x
     8x   6x   5x   6x   2x   2x
1x   2x   11x 2x   4x   2x   1x
          4x   3x   2x   1x
8x   3x   1x   2x   1x
1x   9x   4x   3x   2x   2x   2x
2x   2x   3x   2x   3x   31x 1x
2x   1x   3x   2x   3x   1x
2x   9x   2x   2x   1x   1x   1x   4x
8x   2x   2x   2x   1x
1x   1x   1x   6x   1x
2x   2x   1x   2x
2x   13x 2x   1x   2x   2x
          2x   1x   2x

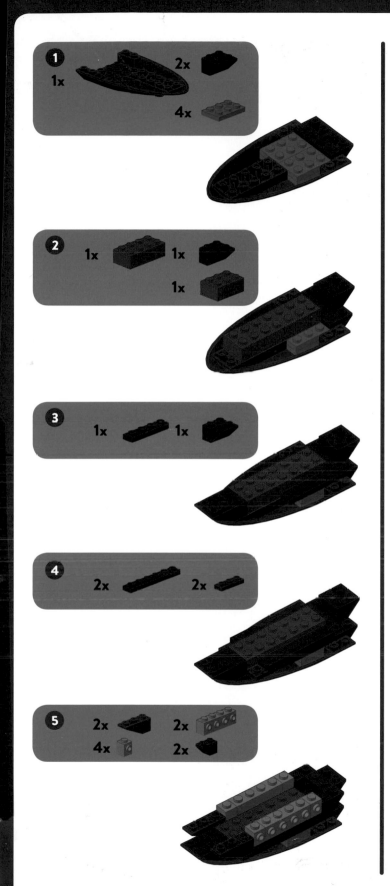

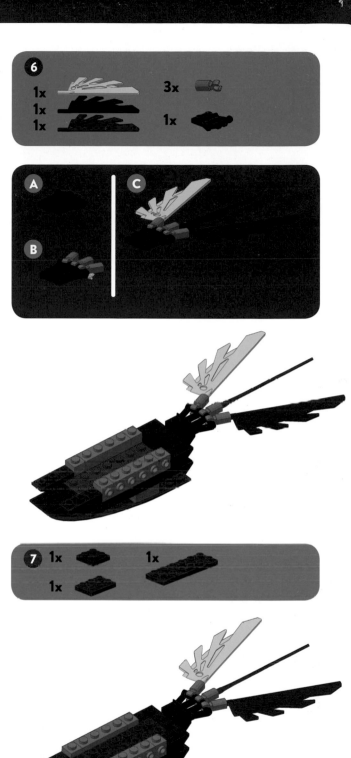

163

8

1x 2x

9

2x 1x 2x
1x 1x 2x
1x 1x 1x

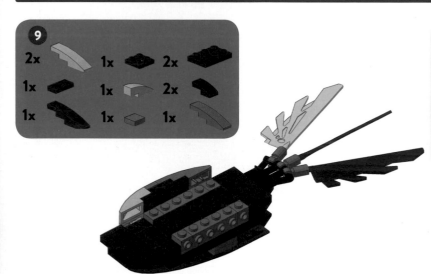

A   C
B   D

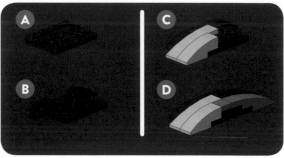

10

2x 1x 2x
1x 1x 2x
1x 1x 1x

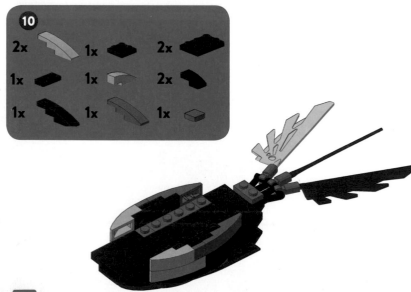

A   C
B   D

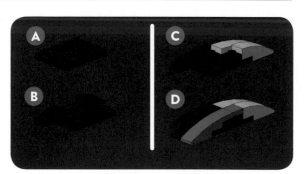

11 2x 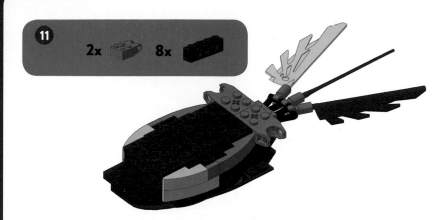 8x

12 1x 4x
1x
4x

A

B

C

D
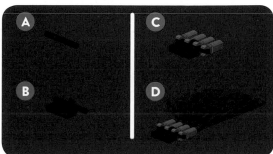

13 1x  2x

14
1x 2x
1x 1x
1x

15
1x 2x
1x 1x

16
2x 2x
1x

17
2x 1x
1x 2x

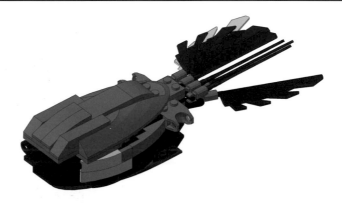

3x 1x 1x 1x 1x 1x 2x 4x 4x

1x 1x 1x

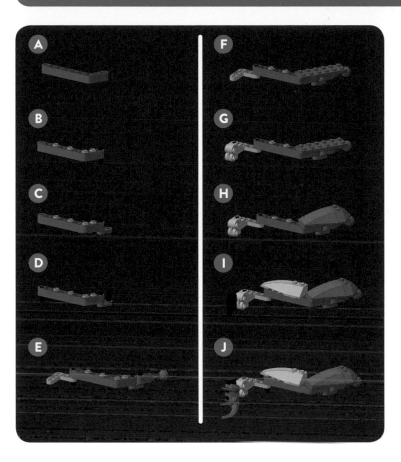

A

B

C

D

E

F

G

H

I

J

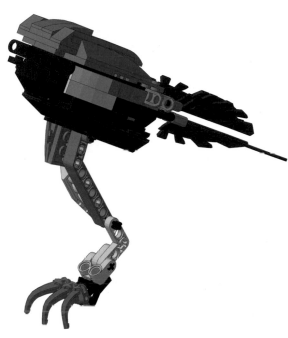

FACT

- Archaeopteryx's name means "ancient feather." It shared characteristics with non-birdlike feathered dinosaurs and with modern birds. Like modern birds, it was feathered and had two broad wings, which would have allowed it to glide and perhaps make short flapping flights. Unlike modern birds, but like many other theropod dinosaurs, Archaeopteryx also had sharp teeth and a long bony tail.

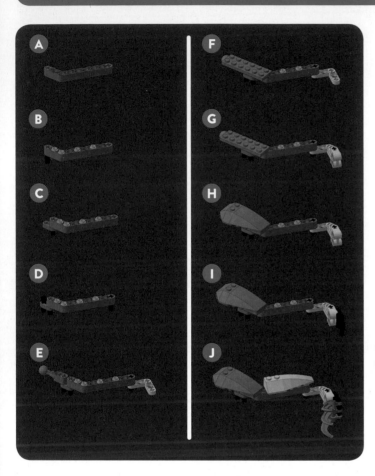

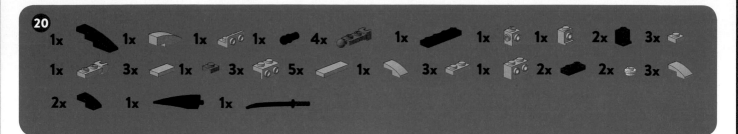

20

PART 1

A

B

C

PART 2

A

B

C

D

E

F

G

H

I

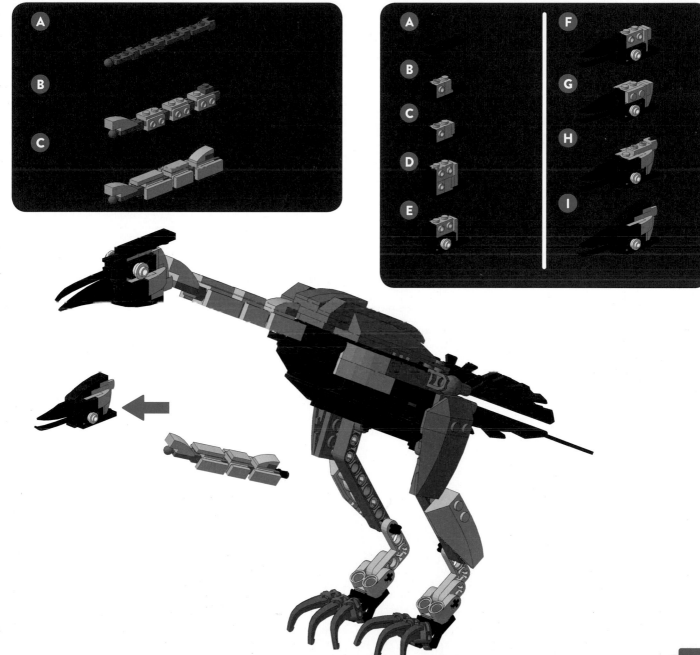

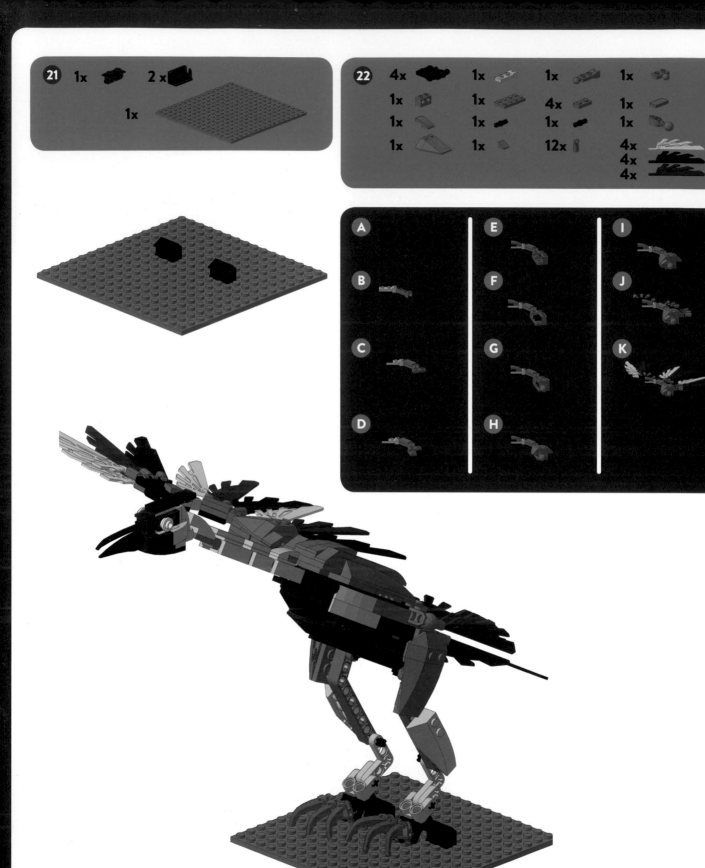

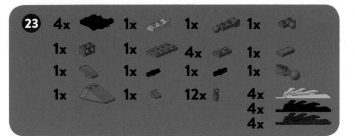

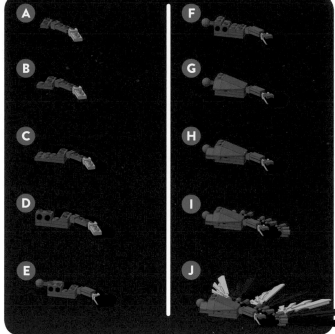

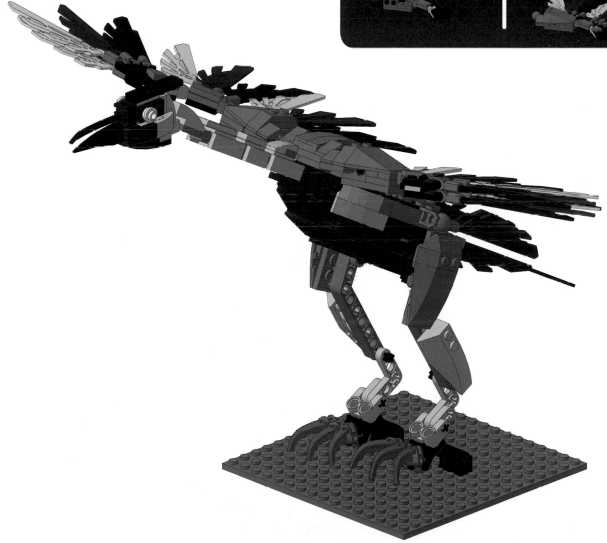

ARCHAEOPTERYX

When Archaeopteryx lived in Germany, Europe was a group of islands in a warm, tropical sea, much closer to the equator than today. Although Archaeopteryx lived among islands, it probably did not eat fish. It likely seized small prey such as lizards, frogs, insects, and mammals with its jaws. Its claws may have been used to pin down larger prey.

PTERANODON

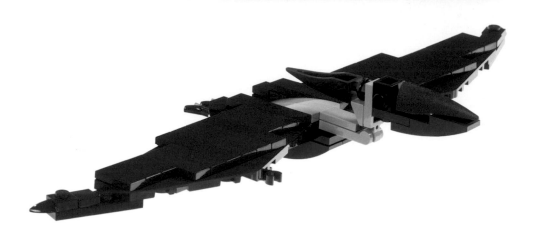

PIECES REQUIRED

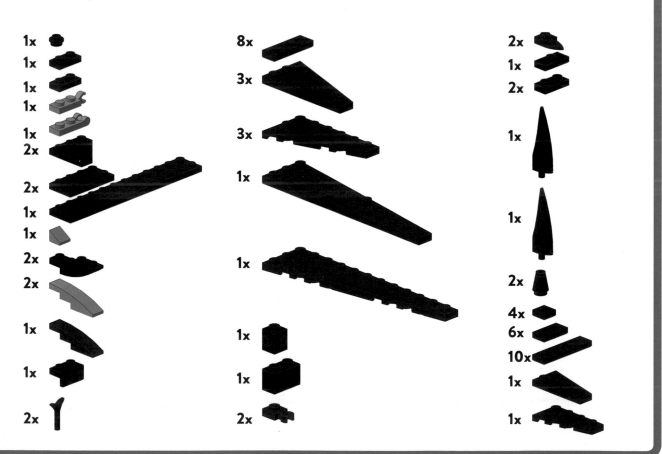

1x	8x	2x
1x	3x	1x
1x		2x
1x	3x	
1x		1x
2x	1x	
2x		1x
1x		
1x	1x	2x
2x		4x
2x		6x
		10x
1x	1x	1x
1x	1x	
2x	2x	1x

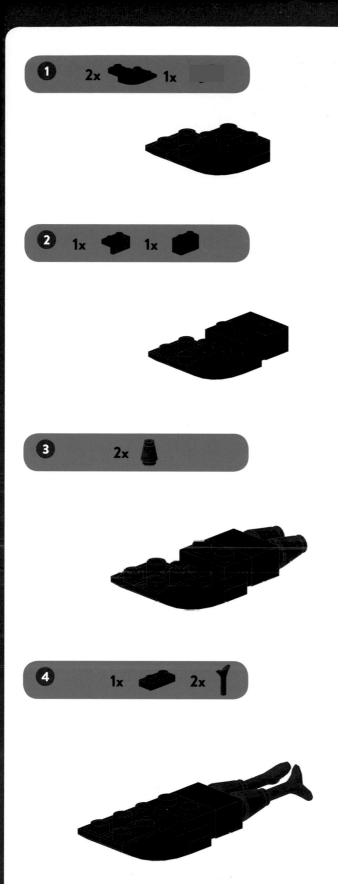

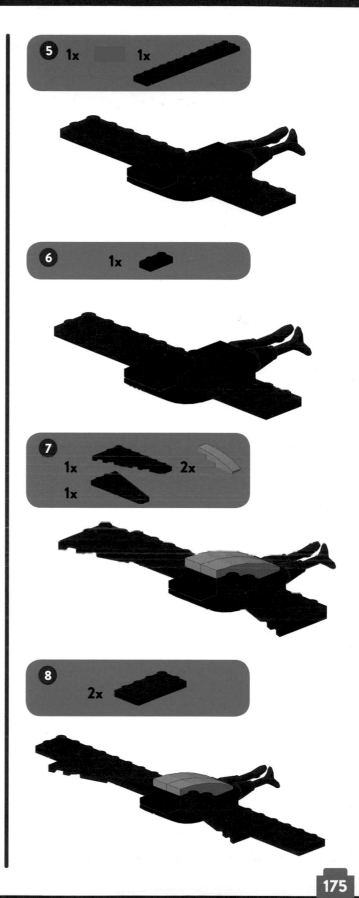

9

1x

1x

2x

2x

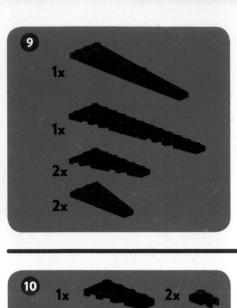
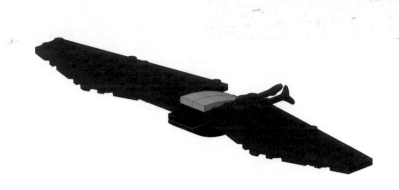

10

1x 2x

1x 2x

11

2x 4x

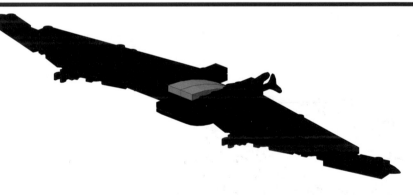

12

8x 10x

6x

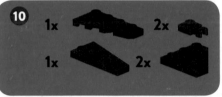
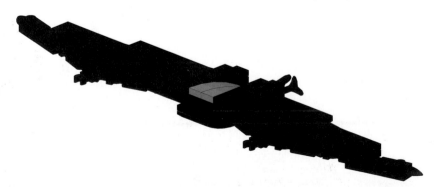

13
1x  1x

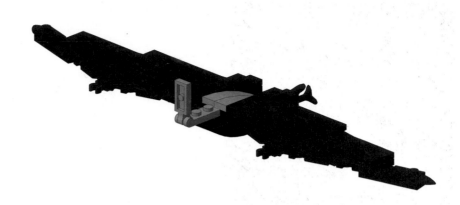

14
1x 1x
1x

15
1x 1x
1x
1x

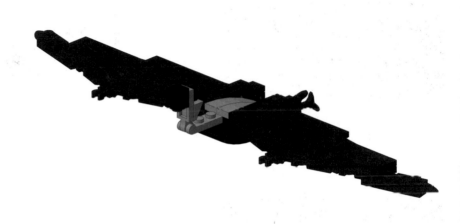

PTERANODON

The Pteranodon is part of a group called pterosaurs. More fossil specimens have been found of the Pteranodon than any other pterosaur. There are more than 1,200 specimens—most of them with nearly complete skulls and skeletons!

DISCOVERING DINOSAURS

Fossils are the remains of dinosaurs, and other animals and plants, that have hardened into rock. Paleontologists are scientists who study dinosaur fossils to discover what they looked like and how they behaved.

HOW A FOSSIL FORMS

Fossils form only when a dinosaur (or other animal or plant) dies in a suitable spot. Fossilization can happen if the body is soon buried in sand or mud, which may happen on a seabed, riverbed, or lakebed. The soft tissues in a dinosaur's body, such as skin and flesh, generally rot or are eaten by scavengers. Over several years, the hard skeleton sinks into the mud. Minerals slowly harden the surrounding mud into rock. They do the same to the minerals in the skeleton and teeth, turning them into stone.

Paleontologists have found dinosaur fossils all over the world.

Although soft tissues usually rot away, sometimes—when the conditions for fossilization were absolutely right—paleontologists do find preserved skin, feathers, and even tendons and ligaments, which join bones together. Fossilized dinosaur eggs have been found, some containing little skeletons. Paleontologists have also found dinosaur footprints, preserved in fossilized mud. These prints are known as trace fossils.

As well as finding fossilized dinosaur skeletons, paleontologists have also found dinosaur tracks, teeth, skeletons of other prehistoic animals, and coprolites— dinosaur poo!

Not all dinosaurs, plants, or animals become fossils when they die. They have to die in the right circumstances, like in a river or the seabed, and not get eaten by another animal before they can be covered in sediment.

1. A dinosaur dies in the right environment.

2. The dinosaur is covered by sand, mud, ice, ash, or other sediments and is left undisturbed.

3. As time goes on, the dinosaur is covered in more sediment.

4. When the right conditions for fossilization occur, sediment seeps into the tiny holes in the bones and forms the fossil.

FINDING FOSSILS

When looking for fossils, paleontologists head for sedimentary rocks, which are formed from layers of sand or mud. Deserts, such as those in western North America, and cliffs, like England's Jurassic Coast, are good places to find exposed fossils. Here, the layers of covering rock have been worn away by waves, wind, or rain. When a fossil is found, the chunks of rock surrounding the bones are carefully photographed, cut out, and taken away. In a research center, the skeleton is reconstructed. Complete skeletons are rarely found, so paleontologists make careful guesses, based on other skeletons and animals alive today, about the missing pieces. They also examine the bones for signs of how they were attached to muscles. This gives them clues about how the animal moved.

Paleontologists used to think that dinosaurs were probably greenish or brownish in color, like many modern reptiles. However, in recent years, fossilized feathers have been found that still contain color pigments. For example, it was discovered that the birdlike theropod Sinosauropteryx was covered in orange feathers and its tail was striped.

People have been finding dinosaur fossils for thousands of years, but they had no idea what they were. The word *dinosaur* was first used in 1842 by the English paleontologist Richard Owen. Understanding of dinosaurs continues to grow and change. It was only in the 1990s that paleontologists found proof that many dinosaurs had feathers.

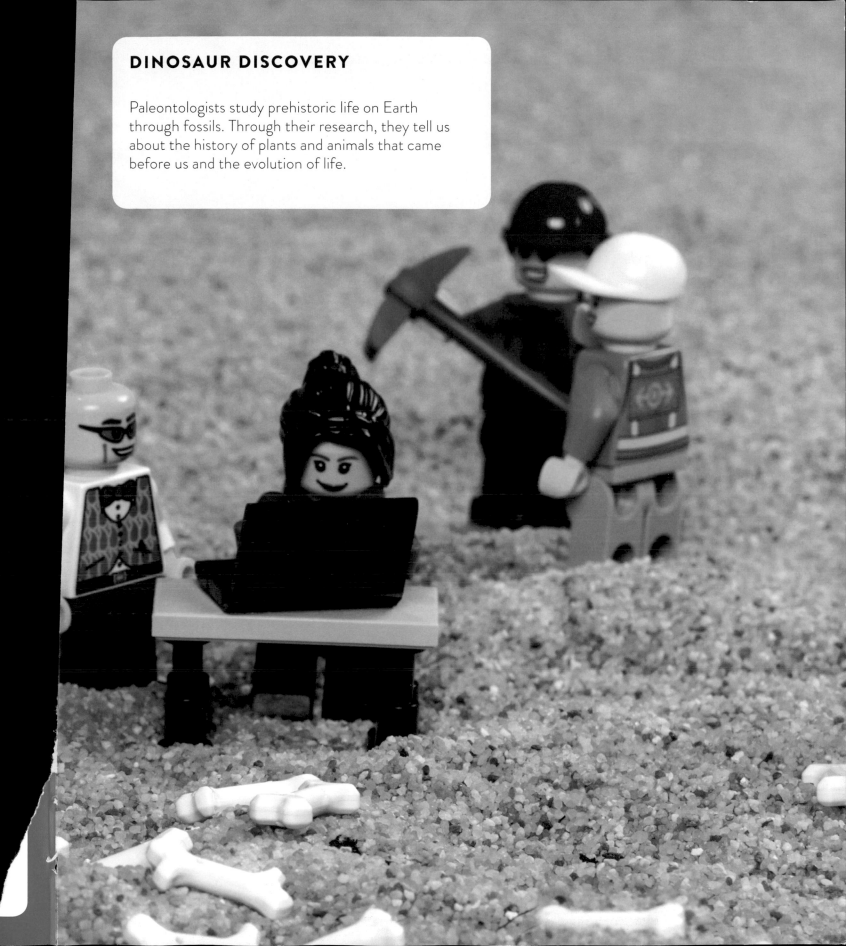

DINOSAUR DISCOVERY

Paleontologists study prehistoric life on Earth through fossils. Through their research, they tell us about the history of plants and animals that came before us and the evolution of life.

BRONTOSAURUS SKELETON

PIECES REQUIRED

1x		1x		13x		4x		1x
6x		10x		21x			
2x		20x		1x		51x		4x
2x		10x		6x		6x		2x
1x		4x		4x		4x		7x
8x		4x		2x		6x		3x
4x		4x				8x		4x
4x		2x				3x		
2x		6x				8x		
2x		3x				4x		
8x		2x				1x		
5x		10x					
14x		2x				4x		

You will also need two pieces of Lego flexitube. This part was originally introduced as part of the Technic range but is now used to add detail to many different models.

2x

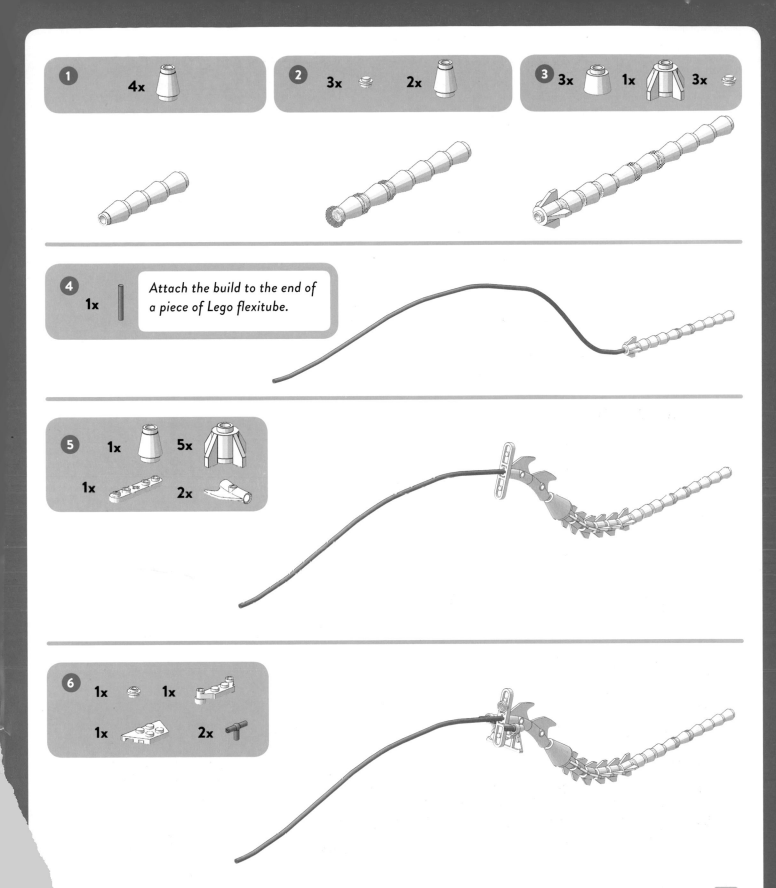

1 4x

2 3x 2x

3 3x 1x 3x

4 1x *Attach the build to the end of a piece of Lego flexitube.*

5 1x 5x
   1x 2x

6 1x 1x
   1x 2x

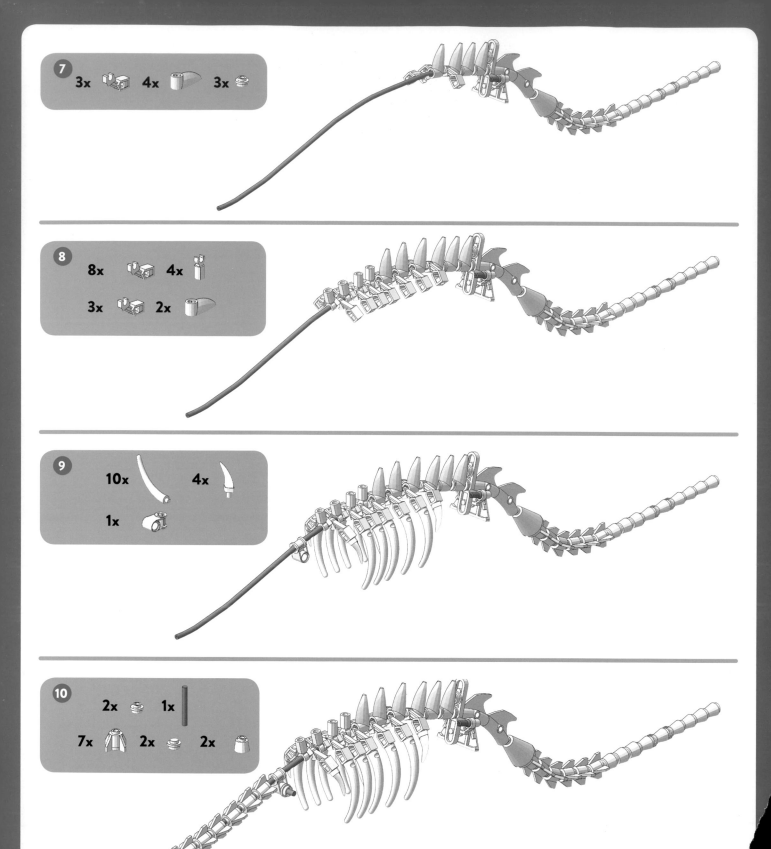

7
3x 4x 3x

8
8x 4x
3x 2x

9
10x 4x
1x

10
2x 1x
7x 2x 2x

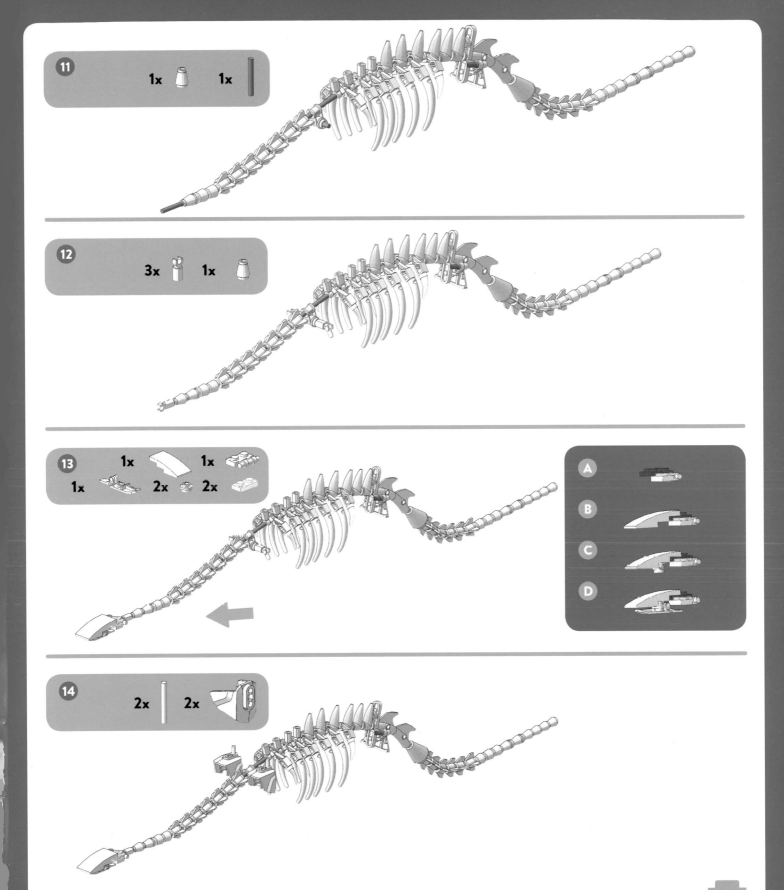

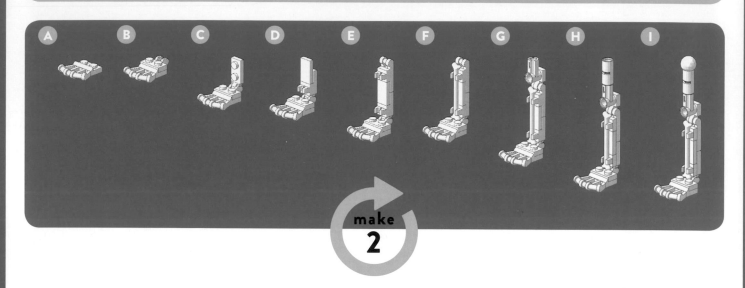

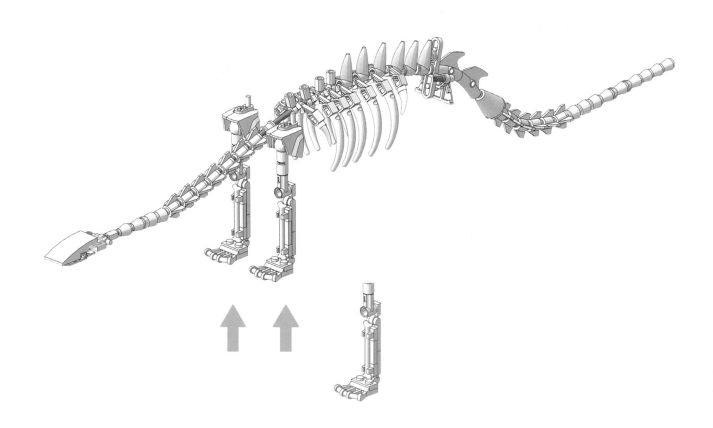

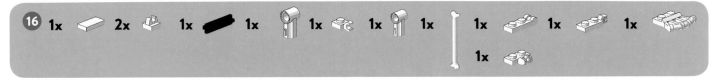

16 1x 2x 1x 1x 1x 1x 1x 1x 1x 1x

1x

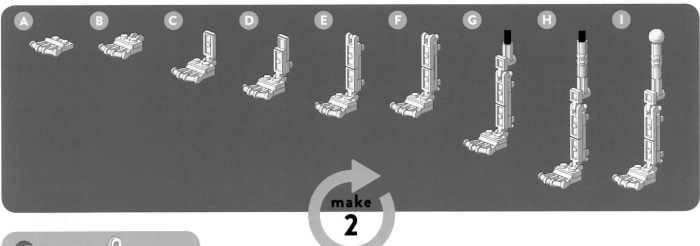

A B C D E F G H I

make
2

17

2x

Attach back legs with this special socket.

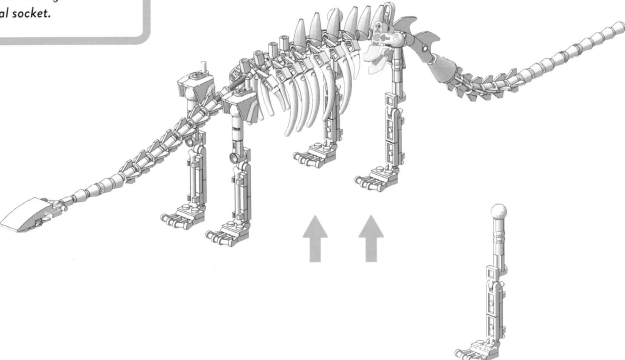

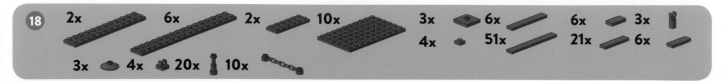

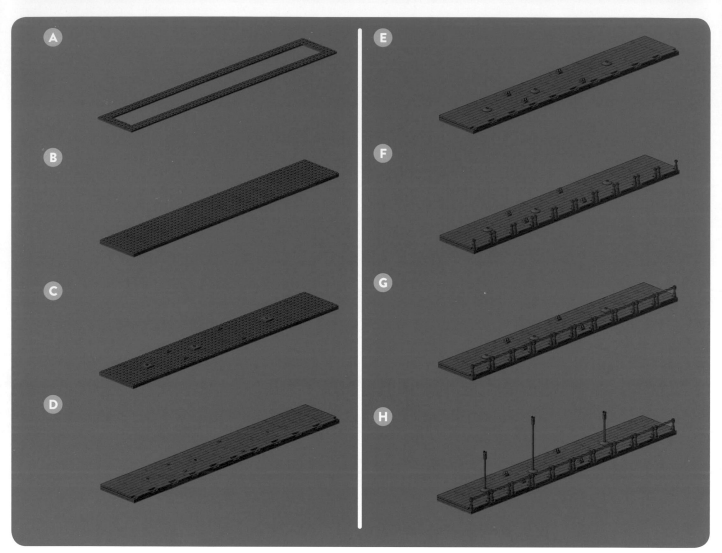

- Large animals are more efficient at getting energy from their food, as it spends longer in their huge digestive systems. This means that large animals can get by on eating much poorer-quality food than smaller animals. Sauropods lived in dry areas and may have evolved to their great size because they needed more energy from the poor-quality plants.

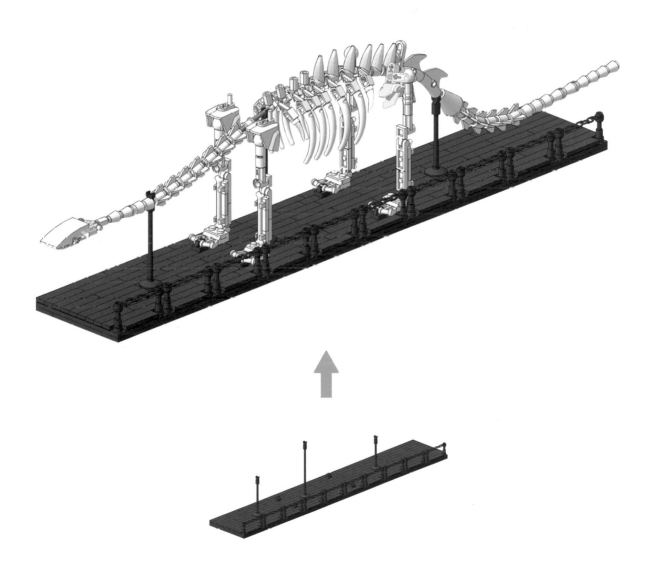

BRONTOSAURUS SKELETON

Brontosaurus was named "thunder lizard" for the sound it must have made as it walked, given it weighed 33 US tons (30 metric tons). Some paleontologists think Brontosaurus is just the same as Apatosaurus and should therefore be known by the same name. Others think there are slight differences between Brontosaurus and Apatosaurus.

DINOSAUR ANATOMY

The smallest known dinosaurs were the size of a chicken, while the heaviest weighed as much as ten African elephants. However, all dinosaurs had certain body features in common. They were all reptiles with four limbs.

SHARED FEATURES

All dinosaurs had four limbs, with their hind legs held straight beneath the body when walking. To allow for this straight-legged gait, dinosaurs had different hip bones from other reptiles. Many dinosaurs walked only on their two hind legs, like birds do today. These dinosaurs usually had shorter front limbs. Other species walked on all four legs, holding them all straight beneath their bodies. That is how mammals such as dogs and cows walk today, but not how other reptiles walk. Some species could switch between two and four legs.

All dinosaurs had a particular form to their skull, with extra holes between the eye sockets and nostrils, and two more behind the eye sockets. Many dinosaurs had body structures that could be used for display, such as crests or horns. Some of these may have been used to attract mates, some to frighten away rivals, and some to startle predators. Fossils have revealed that some dinosaurs were covered in feathers. A few scientists think that all dinosaurs had feathers, or a bristly, feathery fuzz over their skin. Many other scientists think that only some meat-eating dinosaurs had feathers.

TWO GROUPS

There were two major groups of dinosaurs: the ornithischians, which fed only on plants, and the saurischians, which included carnivores and herbivores, as well as modern birds. The main difference between the two groups was the shape of their hip bones. In ornithischians, the pubis bone was below the ischium bone. In saurischians, the pubis bone pointed away from the ischium bone. Ornithischians also had an extra bone in their lower jaw, making it longer. This would have been useful for chewing off leaves and grasses.

Every so often, dinosaur remains will be found with preserved organs, muscles, and skin! Paleontologists will use the latest technology to scan through the rock surrounding them and have learned a lot about dinosaur anatomy this way.

DIFFERENT HIP BONES

Saurischian ("lizard-hipped")

In the saurischian dinosaurs, the pubis pointed forward, helping to support the strong gut muscles.

Ornithischian ("bird-hipped")

In the ornithischian dinosaurs, the pubis bone runs back parallel to the ischium. This allowed the space for the large intestines that the herbivores needed—so that the food could stay in their body for longer, squeezing out as many nutrients as possible.

Even though the ornithischian dinosaurs were called "bird-hipped," birds actually evolved from the saurischian dinosaurs!

Ornithischians included armored dinosaurs such as Stegosaurus and Ankylosaurus, as well as horned dinosaurs such as Triceratops. Other common groups included the duck-billed dinosaurs, named for the flat, duck-like appearance of their mouths. Among these were Corythosaurus and Parasaurolophus.

Saurischian dinosaurs included the gigantic sauropods. These were long-necked and long-tailed plant-eaters. They had small heads, compared to their body size, and walked on four huge, pillar-like legs. Sauropods included Brontosaurus, Brachiosaurus, and Diplodocus. Meat-eaters that ran on their hind legs, called theropods, included the huge Spinosaurus, as well as smaller ostrich-like dinosaurs such as Struthiomimus. Archaeopteryx, an ancestor of modern birds, was also a saurischian meat-eater.

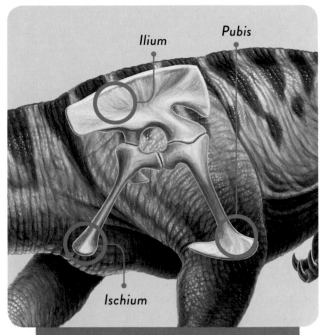

Saurischian dinosaur hip bones, like those of the Allosaurus.

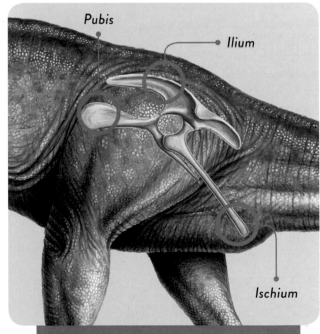

Ornithischian dinosaur hip bones, like those of the Edmontosaurus.

STRUTHOMIMIUS SKELETON

PIECES REQUIRED

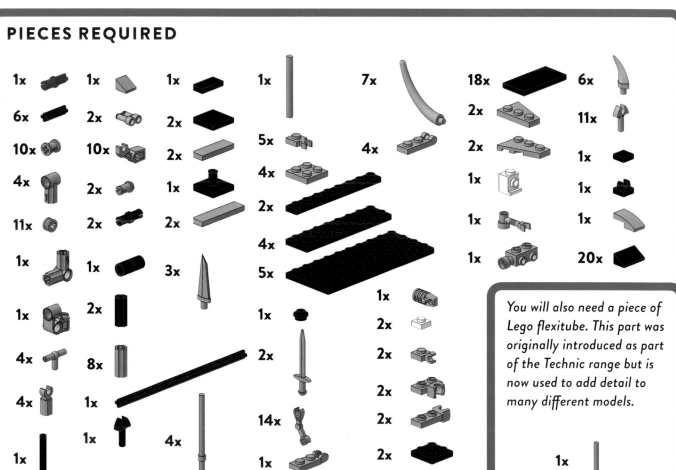

1x   1x   1x   1x   7x   18x   6x

6x   2x   2x   2x   4x   2x   11x

10x   10x   2x   5x   4x   2x   1x

4x   2x   1x   4x   1x   1x

11x   2x   2x   2x   4x   1x   1x

1x   1x   3x   5x   1x   20x

1x   2x   1x   2x

4x   8x   2x   2x

4x   1x   14x   2x

1x   1x   4x   1x   2x

You will also need a piece of Lego flexitube. This part was originally introduced as part of the Technic range but is now used to add detail to many different models.

1x

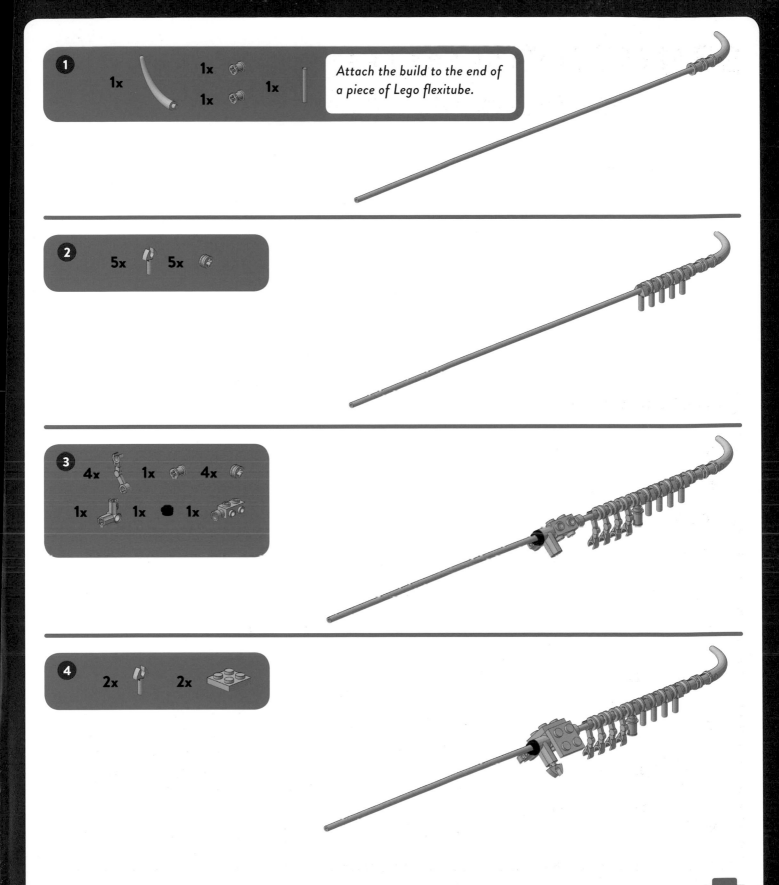

1 1x · 1x · 1x · 1x · *Attach the build to the end of a piece of Lego flexitube.*

2 5x · 5x

3 4x · 1x · 4x · 1x · 1x · 1x

4 2x · 2x

5

2x

2x

2x

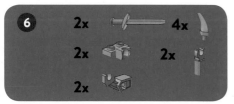

6

2x 4x

2x 2x

2x

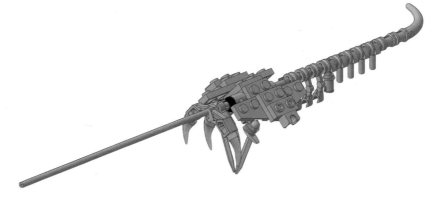

7

6x 2x

4x

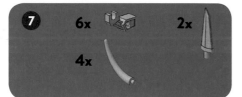

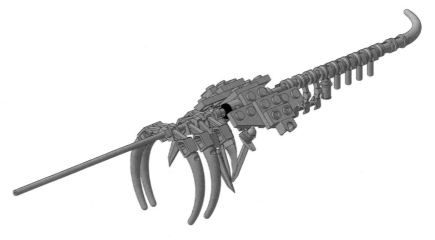

8

1x 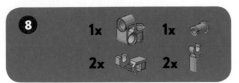 1x

2x 2x

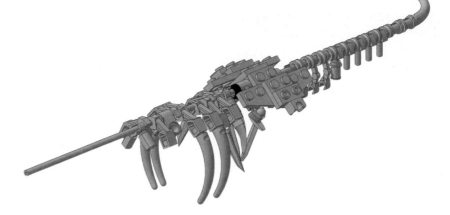

9

8x 2x

2x 2x

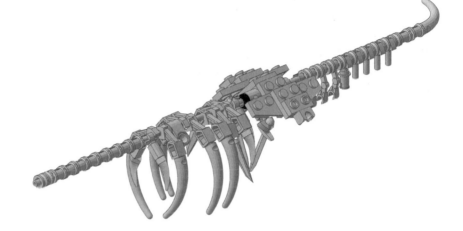

10

1x 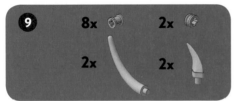 1x

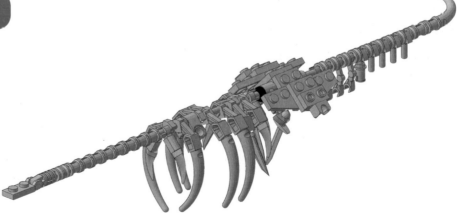

11 2x 🧱 1x ◣

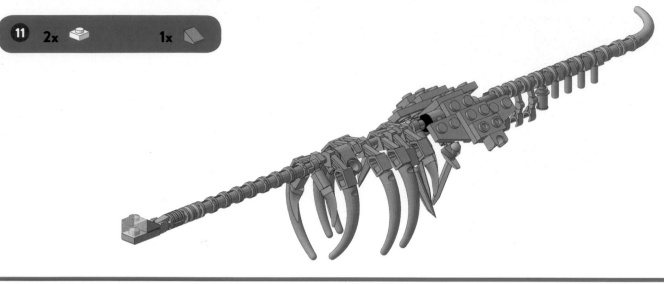

12 1x ◗ 1x 📷
1x 🔧

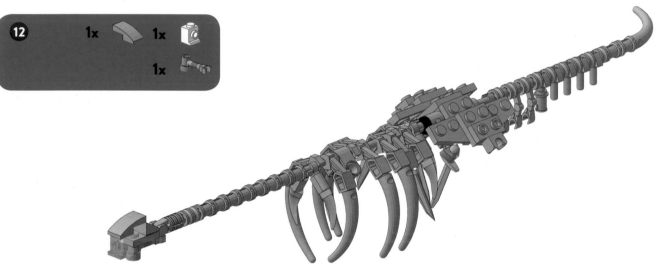

13 3x ▬ 4x ◢
1x 🔩

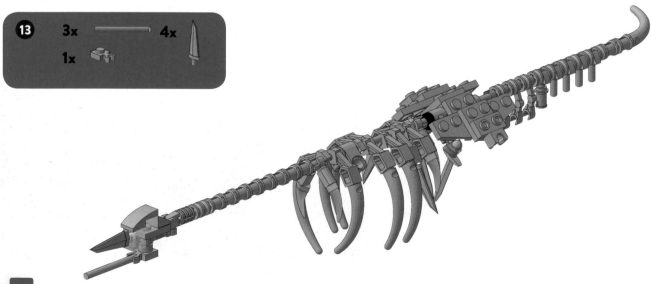

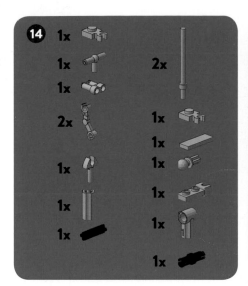

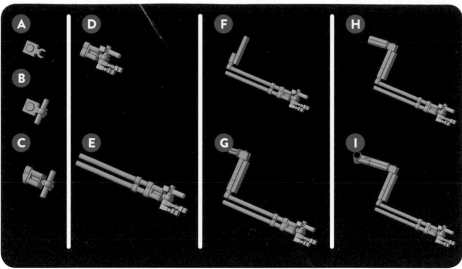

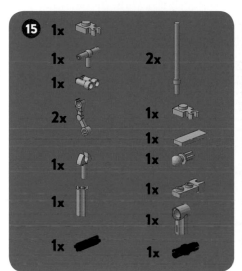

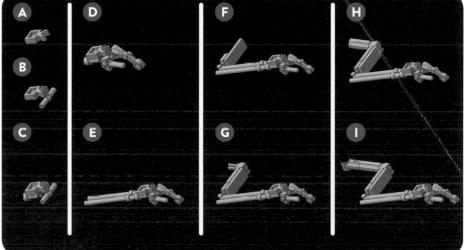

FACT

- Struthiomimus means "ostrich mimic" because of this dinosaur's similar appearance to modern ostriches. It was 14 feet (4.5 m) long from beak to tip of tail, longer than a modern ostrich largely because of its tail. It weighed about 330 pounds (150 kg), slightly more than a male ostrich or as much as two adult men. Ostriches can run at up to 42 miles (70 km) per hour, and Struthiomimus may have been similarly speedy.

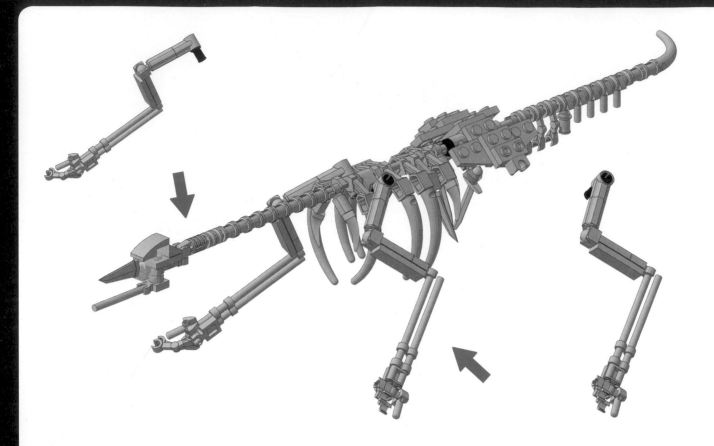

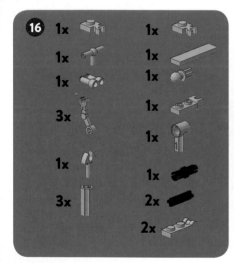

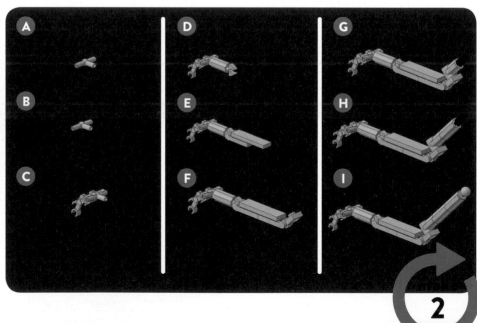

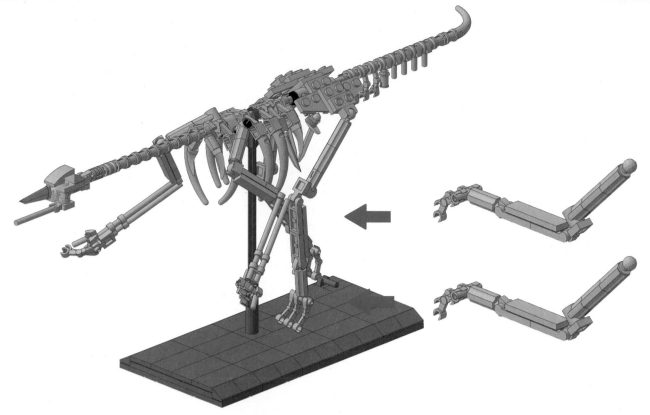

5x · 1x
2x · 1x
4x · 1x
2x · 1x
1x
20x

1x · 1x
18x · 2x
1x · 1x
1x

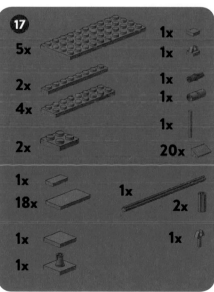

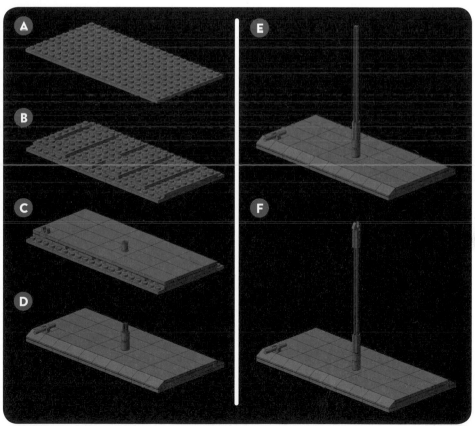

A

B

C

D

E

F

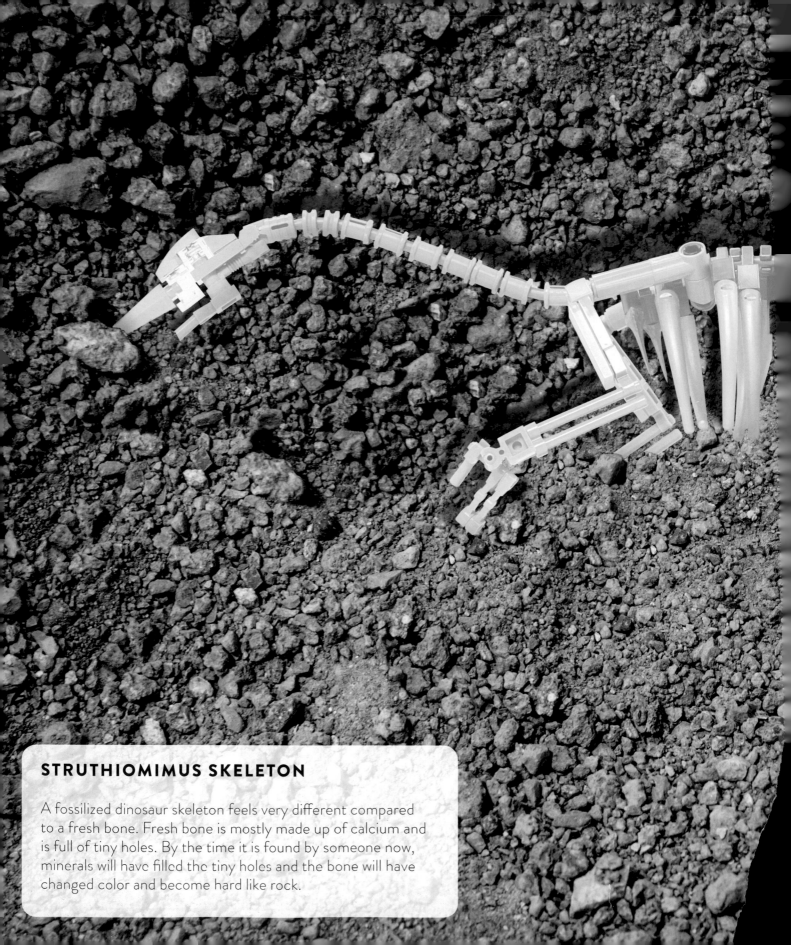

STRUTHIOMIMUS SKELETON

A fossilized dinosaur skeleton feels very different compared to a fresh bone. Fresh bone is mostly made up of calcium and is full of tiny holes. By the time it is found by someone now, minerals will have filled the tiny holes and the bone will have changed color and become hard like rock.

STRUTHIOMIMUS

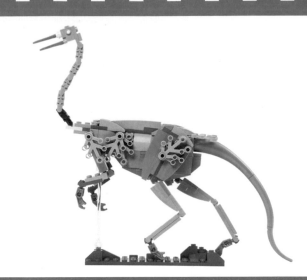

PIECES REQUIRED

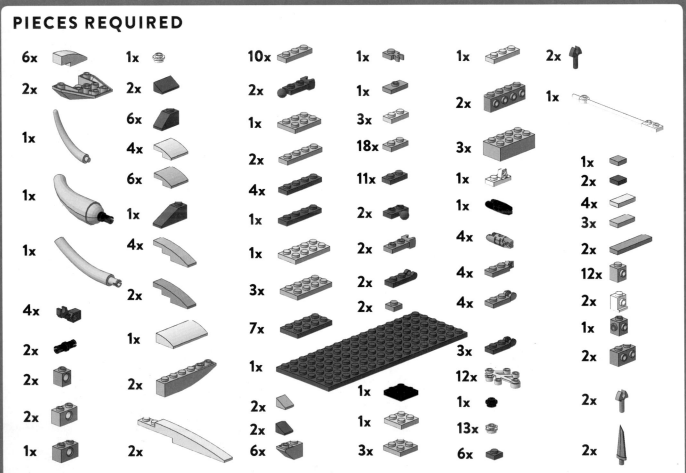

6x

2x

1x

1x

1x

4x

2x

2x

2x

1x

1x

2x

6x

4x

6x

1x

4x

2x

1x

2x

2x

10x

2x

1x

2x

4x

1x

1x

3x

7x

1x

2x

2x

6x

1x

1x

3x

18x

11x

2x

2x

2x

2x

1x

1x

3x

1x

1x

3x

2x

3x

1x

1x

4x

4x

4x

3x

12x

1x

13x

6x

1x

2x

2x

2x

1x

1x

1x

2x

4x

3x

2x

12x

2x

1x

2x

2x

2x

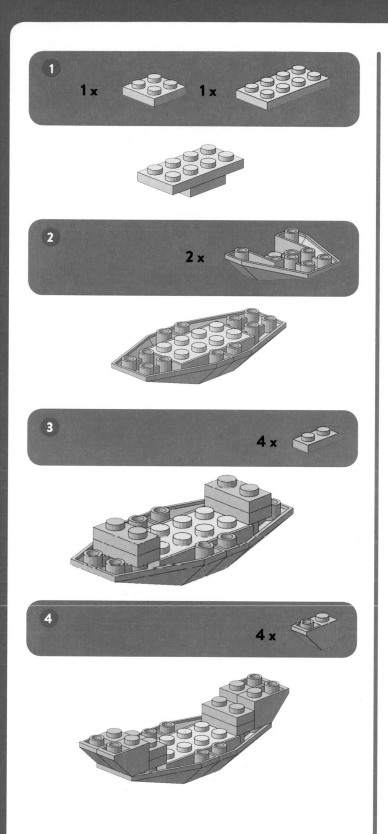

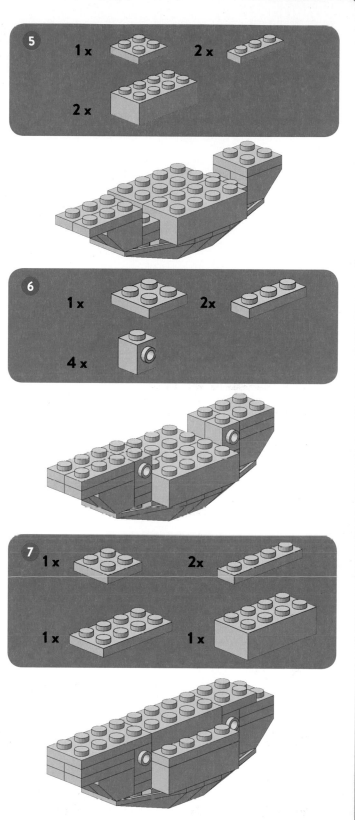

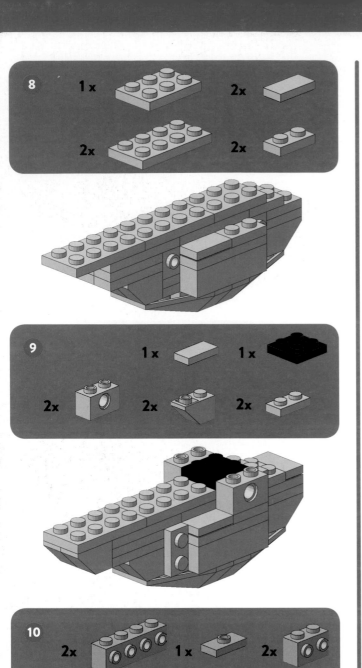

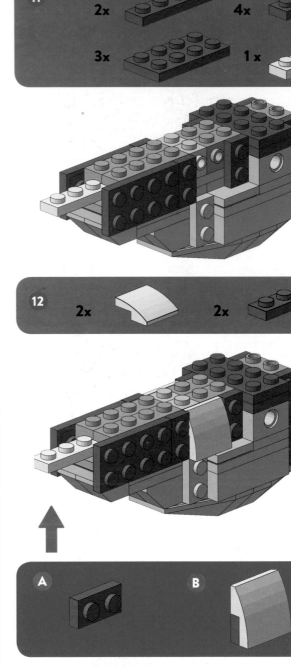

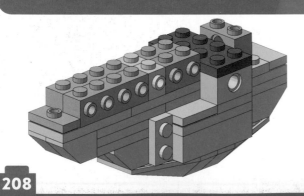

13

2x  2x 1x

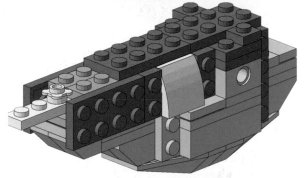

14

1x 2x 1x

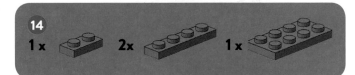

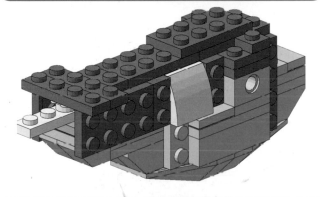

15

2x 2x

2x

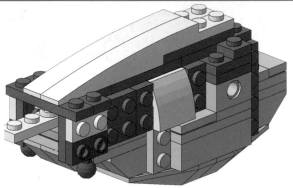

16

6x  1x

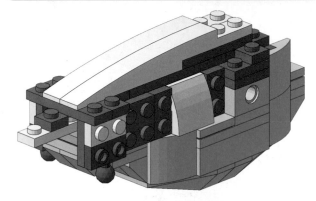

17

2x 1x

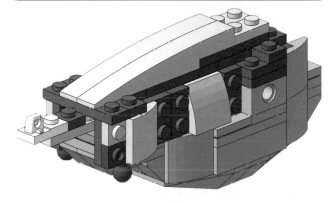

18

4x  1x

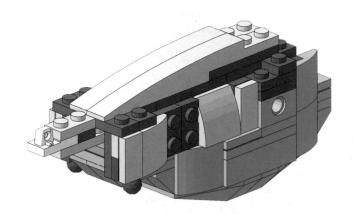

19

2x  2x

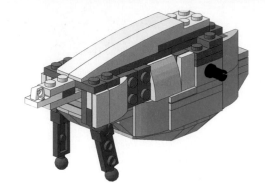

21

1x 2x 10x

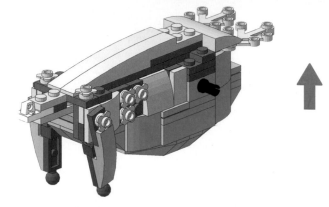

20

2x  2x

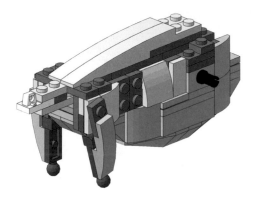

22

4x

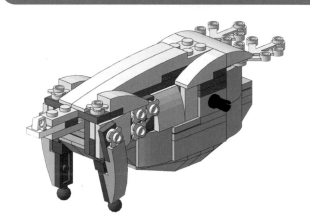

FACT

- Paleontologists are not sure what Struthiomimus ate with its toothless beak. It may have been an omnivore, feeding on plants, insects, and small fish or land animals. However, some Paleontologists think its hands were not suited to grasping wriggling prey, so it may have been only an herbivore, using its fingers as simple hooks to bring branches close enough to bite.

2x

2x

2x

2x

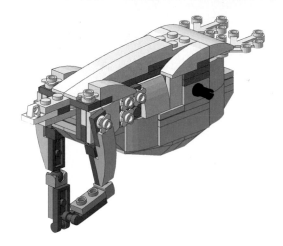

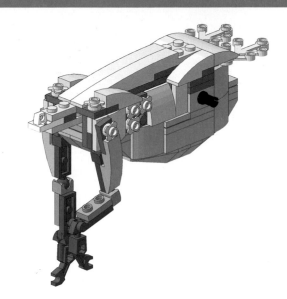

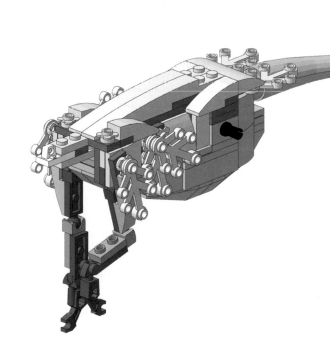

25

1x

1x

1x

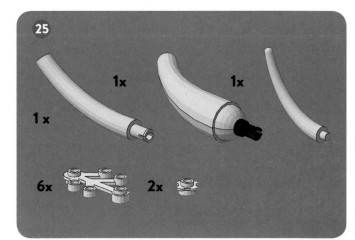

6x

2x

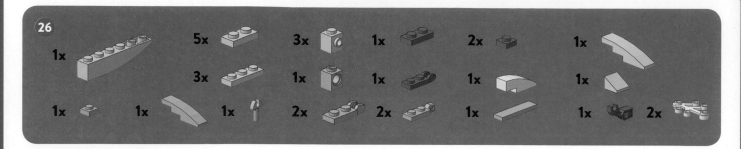

PART 1

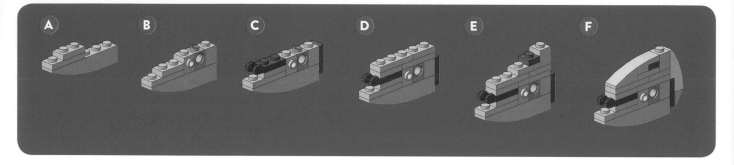

PART 2

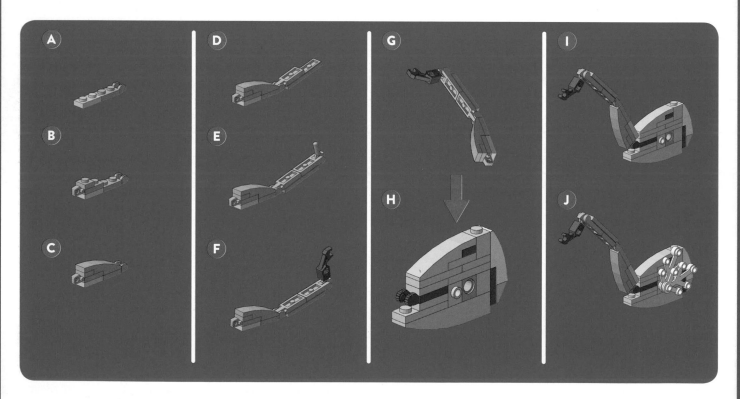

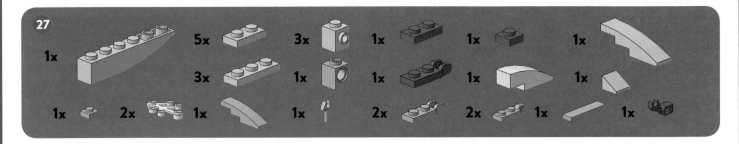

PART 1

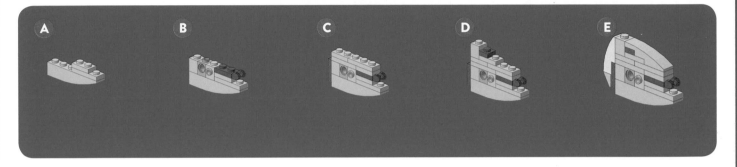

PART 2

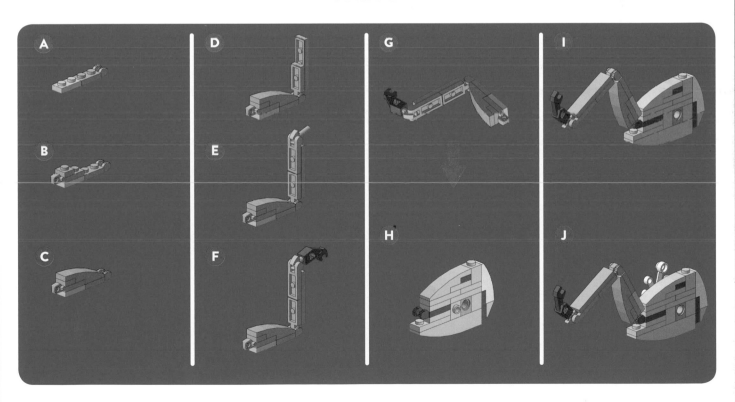

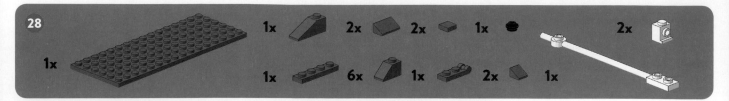

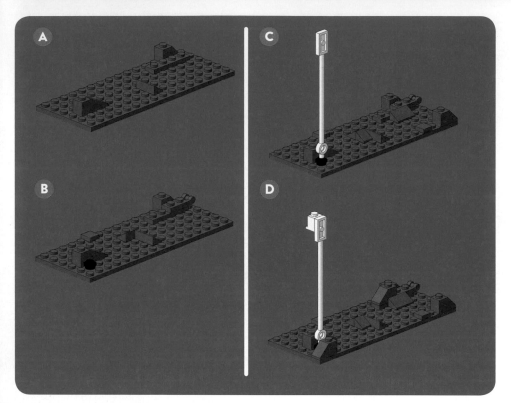

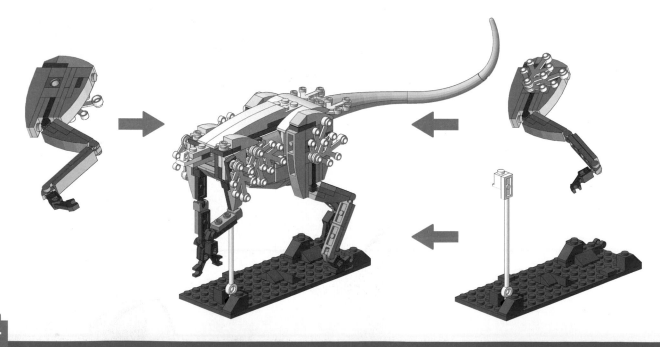

1x 1x 1x 1x 1x 2x 4x 1x

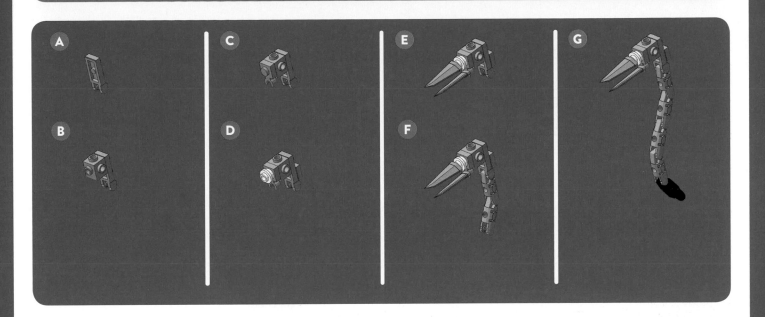

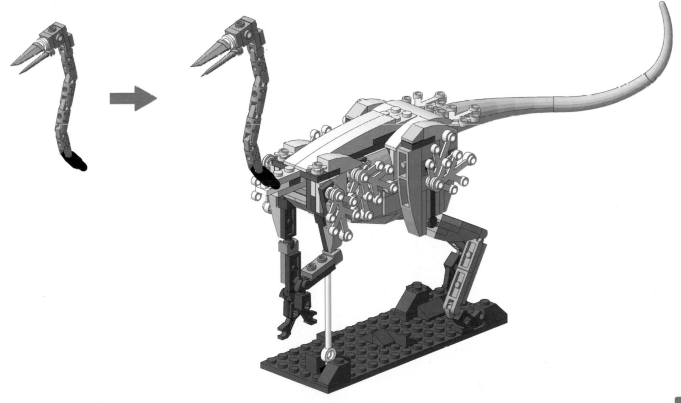

STRUTHIOMIMUS

There has been some debate over the diet of the Struthiomimus. Its straight-edged beak has led some paleontologists to suggest that it may have eaten plants, but others think that it is more likely to be a carnivore because it is classified in the otherwise meat-eating therapod group. At this time, it is thought that the Struthiomimus was an omnivore, eating both meat and plants.

GLOSSARY

Ankylosaurids
A group of plant-eating dinosaurs, such as Euoplocephalus, that lived worldwide. They were heavily armored with thick plates of bone, spikes, and bony skin. They had thick skulls and clubs of solid bone on their tails.

Carnivore
An animal that eats meat.

Carnosaurs
A primitive group of non-feathered, massive, powerful, meat-eating theropod dinosaurs, such as Allosaurus and Giganotosaurus. They were predators as well as scavengers.

Coelurosaurs
The largest group of the meat-eating dinosaurs. They were most common during the Cretaceous period and birds evolved from them. All feathered dinosaurs and tyrannosaurs are in this group.

Continent
A large area of continental crust with a surface that is above sea level. There are seven continents on Earth: Africa, Antarctica, Asia, Australia, Europe, North America, South America.

Coprolite
Fossilized poo.

Cretaceous Period
The third and last geological period of the Mesozoic Era, when many dinosaurs evolved and then became extinct. It lasted from 144 to 65 million years ago.

Era
A division of time in Earth's history. Geologists divide eras into periods.

Extinction
The dying out of a species, or of large communities of animals and plants (called a mass extinction). Mesozoic dinosaurs became extinct at the end of the Cretaceous. Their descendants, the birds, did not.

Fossil
The preserved remains or traces of plants or animals. These were buried and then turned to stone or left their impression on rock.

Hadrosaurs
Duck-billed, plant-eating dinosaurs, such as Parasaurolophus. They had broad, duck-like beaks, grinding teeth, and many had bony head crests. They evolved in Asia during the early Cretaceous before spreading to Europe and the Americas.

Herbivore
An animal that eats only plants.

Ichthyosaurs
A group of dolphin-like marine reptiles that lived at the same time as the dinosaurs. They gave birth to live young in the sea.

Iguanodontians
Large, plant-eating ornithopod dinosaurs, such as Iguanodon, that mostly walked on four feet. They first appeared during the Jurassic Period and became widespread during the Early Cretaceous Period.

Jurassic Period
The middle geological period of the Mesozoic Era. It lasted from 208 to 144 million years ago. The conditions on Earth were just right for new kinds of dinosaurs to flourish, particularly the huge, long-necked sauropods.

Mammals
A group of animals that have backbones as well as hair or fur and feed their young on milk. Humans are mammals, as are dogs, cats, and bats.

Mesozoic Era
The Age of Dinosaurs. It began about 250 million years ago, before dinosaurs had evolved, and ended about 65 million years ago with a mass extinction. It spanned the Triassic, Jurassic, and Cretaceous Periods.

Mosaurs

An extinct group of large marine lizards also known as "sea dragons." They lived in inshore waters during the Late Cretaceous. They had eel-shaped bodies with four flippers.

Omnivore

An animal that eats both prey animals and plant matter.

Ornithopods

"Bird-footed," two-legged ornithischian dinosaurs. This group included the hadrosaurs and iguanodontians.

Paleontologist

A scientist who studies ancient life, especially the fossils of plants and animals.

Pangea

The super-continent linking all the modern continents. It formed in the Permian Period and started to break up during the Triassic.

Period

A standard division of time in Earth's history that is shorter than an era.

Plesiosaurs

Large, fish-eating marine reptiles that flourished during the Jurassic and Cretaceous. Their long necks could rise above the sea's surface. They swam through the water using their four paddle-like flippers.

Pterosaurs

Flying reptiles, only distantly related to dinosaurs. Pterosaurs evolved during the late Triassic Period and had wingspans ranging from 1 foot (30 cm) to 45 feet (14 m).

Reptiles

A group of animals that have backbones and scaly skin, and their young hatch out of shelled eggs. Snakes, lizards, and crocodiles are modern reptiles.

Sauropods

A group of four-legged saurischian dinosaurs with long necks and tails, such as Diplodocus. They had lizard-like hips, while most other plant eaters had birdlike hips. Evolving in the late Triassic, they included the largest animals ever to walk on Earth.

Spinosaurs

A group of "sail-backed" Cretaceous theropod dinosaurs with enlarged thumb-claws and long, thin, crocodile-like snouts.

Stegosaurs

Four-legged, plant-eating dinosaurs with bony plates along their backs and long, sharp spikes on their strong tails. From the late Jurassic period, they roamed North America, Europe, Asia, and Africa, and included Stegosaurus.

Theropods

All the meat-eating dinosaurs. They were lizard-hipped and walked on their back legs.

Triassic Period

The first geological period in the Mesozoic era, from 245 to 208 million years ago. Dinosaurs appeared about halfway through this period, around 228 million years ago.

Trilobite

Small crablike creatures with three body parts that lived in the seas. Trilobites became extinct at the end of the Permian, just before the Age of Dinosaurs.

Tyrannosaurs

A group of theropod dinosaurs such as Albertosaurus. They are all related to the last member of their group, Tyrannosaurus.

INDEX

ABOUT THE AUTHOR

DO YOU REALLY BUILD LEGO® MODELS FOR A LIVING?

It's a question I'm asked again and again, and the answer is yes. I really do build LEGO® models for a living and it's a pretty good job! I think what people really would like to know, though, is how I ended up with this job and what we really do, day-in and day-out. So, this is the story!

As a child, I was always interested in LEGO® sets. Each January, I would get hold of the latest catalog and look at all the new sets that were going to be released that year. I'd decide which ones I'd ask my parents for on my birthday—and which sets I'd ask Father Christmas if he could find for me. Usually I was very lucky and I built up a huge LEGO® collection. Like most children at that time, though, come the age of 15 or 16, I put my LEGO® aside and became more interested in other things!

I came back to LEGO® in my mid-20s. In 2000, The LEGO® Group released a Statue of Liberty model and again, I was bought a LEGO® set as a gift. That set kicked my interest back into action, and I quickly became an "Adult Fan of LEGO®." As an AFOL, I built models of things that I knew and eventually I started being asked to build models for other people. In 2012, I was lucky enough to be asked by Visit Denmark (the Danish tourist board) and LEGO® themselves to build something to commemorate the London Olympics. At the same time, I was in the middle of writing my very first book and quickly I had more LEGO® "work" than real work. So I took the plunge!

Since I started building LEGO® models full time, things have grown very rapidly. My company now has four employees (including me) and we operate from a small studio just outside of Edinburgh, Scotland. Sadly, we don't get to build something every day, but when we do, our studio is organized perfectly to let us build whatever we need. In the center of our building space is a large table. A very large table! It seems that whatever we build from LEGO® needs lots and lots of space.

Lining the two long walls on either side of our studio are racks and racks of drawers. So that we can build anything, we try to keep a very good stock of pieces available. Along one side of the studio are the basics—bricks, plates, and tiles. Down the other side are all the "specials." Slopes, rounds, parts with bars, parts with clips—they are all here. Each drawer is then subdivided with small tubs. So a drawer of 2x2 round plates might have drawers of red, white, yellow parts, etc.

We keep about 4 million elements in stock at any one time and everything has its place! We've found that being ultra-organized has doubled the speed at which we can build models, which is handy when you have more than 30 models to build for one book!

While sometimes we have the liberty of choosing what to build, or how to build it, there are times when our models have to be extremely precise. If this is the case, then often we don't start with LEGO® bricks at all. The first stage is on computer. Building digitally lets me work on a design that might be too large to test in real life, too complex, or just far too awkward! Using a specific LEGO® computer-aided design package, I can create models that don't have to worry about gravity just yet. We can then work on these until it's finally time to work out how to put those bricks together so they do actually fit!

So it's true, I do get paid to build LEGO® models for a living and it is my dream job. I will just sound a word of warning, though—it doesn't mean that you don't have to go to school or get any qualifications! Just like any career, to do my job, I need a good selection of skills. Not only do I have to build with LEGO®, but I also need to be able to use 3-D CAD programs, make calculations about size and volume, write business proposals, and even balance the books! A good base in math, geometry, IT, and English are all essential skills. Art and design helps, too, though I'll admit I am terrible with a pencil!

CREDITS

Warren Elsmore is an artist in LEGO® bricks and a lifelong fan of LEGO® who is based in Edinburgh, United Kingdom. He has been in love with the little plastic bricks since the age of four and now spends his days creating amazing models out of LEGO® bricks.

In 2012, after 15 years in a successful IT career, Warren moved to working full time with LEGO® bricks. Warren's bestselling first book (*Brick City*) was released in 21 languages to critical acclaim and has been followed by a range of books each re-creating parts of the world we inhabit in plastic bricks.

Exhibitions of Warren's first two books (*Brick City* and *Brick Wonders*) have toured museums and galleries throughout the United Kingdom, entertaining hundreds of thousands. His team have broken two Guinness World Records with LEGO® bricks, and in 2015 Warren co-launched "BRICK"—the largest LEGO® fan event in the United Kingdom and one of the largest in the world.

For more information, please visit www.*warrenelsmore.com*.

Jessica Farrell worked on the incredible dinosaur models in this book. She is a freelance LEGO® artist with a lifelong passion for the brick. She loves the endless possibilities of LEGO® and thus embraces all themes with enthusiasm.

From an early age, Jessica's mother taught her an artist's appreciation of color, form, detail, and beauty, which is reflected in her brick work.

Living in County Kildare, Ireland, Jessica runs a garden nursery and smallholding with her family. Despite this busy schedule, she is very active in the LEGO® fan community and regularly exhibits her creations internationally.

Jessica is known online as Janet VanD. Samples of her ealier work can be viewed at *http://janetvand.deviantart.com/gallery/*

Dinosaur text written by **Fay Evans** and **Claudia Martin**, with **Dougal Dixon** as our Dinosaur Consultant.

PICTURE CREDITS

All images not listed (right) are copyright Weldon Owen Pty Ltd.

While every effort has been made to credit all contributors, Weldon Owen would like to apologize should there have been any omissions or errors and would be pleased to make any appropriate corrections for future editions of this book.

P. 16 seeshooteatrepeat/Shutterstock.com, **P. 17** mopic/Shutterstock.com, **P. 31** Sementer/Shutterstock.com **P. 34** Rashevskyi/Shutterstock.com, **P. 35** billysfam/Shutterstock.com, **P. 39** Jaroslav Moravcik/Shutterstock.com, **P. 64 Valentyna Chukhlyebova, P. 65, 120 BL, 120 TR** Hershel Hoffmeyer/Shutterstock.com, **P. 121** Kostyantyn Ivanyshen/Shutterstock.com, **P. 131** Elenarts/Shuttrstock.com, **P. 130 TR** Catmando/Shutterstock.com, **P. 131, 152 TR, 153** Michael Rosskothen/Shutterstock.com, **P. 152 BL** Ralf Juergen Kraft/Shutterstock.com, **P. 180 BL** mj007/Shutterstock.com, **P. 180 BR** Geologist Natural Pics/Shutterstock.com, **P. 182** Panupong Ponchai/Shutterstock.com, **P. 194** Marques/Shutterstock.com